Contents

The Economic and Budgetary Effects of Producing Oil and Natural Gas From Shale

Summary

Recent advances in combining two drilling techniques, hydraulic fracturing and horizontal drilling, have allowed access to large deposits of shale resources—that is, crude oil and natural gas trapped in shale and certain other dense rock formations.[1] As a result, the cost of that "tight oil" and "shale gas" has become competitive with the cost of oil and gas extracted from other sources. Virtually nonexistent a decade ago, the development of shale resources has boomed in the United States, producing about 3.5 million barrels of tight oil per day and about 9.5 trillion cubic feet (Tcf) of shale gas per year. Those amounts equal about 30 percent of U.S. production of liquid fuels (which include crude oil, biofuels, and natural gas liquids) and 40 percent of U.S. production of natural gas. Shale development has also affected the federal budget, chiefly by increasing tax revenues.

The production of tight oil and shale gas will continue to grow over the next 10 years—by about 30 percent and about 60 percent, respectively, according to a recent projection by the Energy Information Administration (EIA).[2] Another EIA estimate shows that the amount of tight oil and shale gas in the United States that could be extracted with today's technology would satisfy domestic oil consumption at current rates for approximately 8 years and domestic gas consumption for 25.[3]

How Will Shale Development Affect Energy Markets?

Total domestic production of oil and natural gas will continue to be higher than it would have been without shale development, reducing the prices of those energy supplies. The lower prices, in turn, will increase domestic consumption of oil and gas, domestic consumption of energy overall, and net exports of gas, while decreasing the production of oil and gas from conventional resources, net imports of oil, and the use of competing fuels.

Shale gas has affected energy prices in the United States more strongly than tight oil has, and it will continue to do so. Indeed, the Congressional Budget Office (CBO) estimates that if shale gas did not exist, the price of natural gas would be about 70 percent higher than currently projected by 2040—whereas if tight oil did not exist, the price of oil would be only about 5 percent higher. One reason for the difference is that shale gas is more plentiful than tight oil, relative to the size of their domestic markets. Another is that the North American market for natural gas is relatively insulated from conditions elsewhere by high transportation costs, so the effects of higher or lower domestic production on market prices are concentrated within the continent; oil, by contrast, is heavily traded in a worldwide market that diffuses the effects of domestic production on prices. (Oil prices are thus influenced by events that occur elsewhere in the world. For example, the recent sharp drop in crude oil prices—as of the end of November 2014, they had dropped about

---

1. For convenience, the term "shale resources" in this report includes energy supplies contained by formations of low-permeability rock that is not shale, such as limestone and fine-grained sandstone.

2. Energy Information Administration, *Annual Energy Outlook 2014 With Projections to 2040*, DOE/EIA-0383(2014) (April 2014), http://go.usa.gov/8KyF (PDF, 12 MB).

3. Those estimates are based on Energy Information Administration, *Technically Recoverable Shale Oil and Shale Gas Resources: An Assessment of 137 Shale Formations in 41 Countries Outside the United States* (June 2013), www.eia.gov/analysis/studies/worldshalegas/; and on Louis Sahagun, "U.S. Officials Cut Estimate of Recoverable Monterey Shale Oil by 96%," *Los Angeles Times* (May 20, 2014), http://tinyurl.com/pnknuct.

one-third from their recent peak in June—was caused not by any sudden or dramatic increase in the supply of tight oil during that period but by other factors, such as a rapid increase in Libyan production and a slowdown of consumption in Europe and Asia.)

EIA's projections of the development of shale resources are the most detailed currently available, and CBO considers them an appropriate basis for estimating the potential economic and budgetary effects of shale development. Nonetheless, like all projections of the future, they are subject to significant uncertainty. Many factors contribute to the uncertainty; for example, the abundance of shale resources, the fraction of those resources that will be recoverable with evolving technology, and the costs of recovering that fraction are not known for certain. Projections of more or less shale development would lead to larger or smaller estimates of the economic and budgetary effects.

How Will Shale Development Affect Economic Output?
The technological innovations behind hydraulic fracturing and horizontal drilling make existing labor and capital—whether they are employed in shale development, in industries using natural gas or oil, or in industries using products derived from natural gas or oil—more productive than they otherwise would be. That heightened productivity has increased gross domestic product (GDP) and will continue to do so.

Shale development also boosts GDP in other ways. The increase in GDP just described represents increased income, which allows people and firms to save and invest more in productive capital, and the higher productivity just described increases wages, raising the amount of labor available. Both the increased capital and the increased labor raise GDP. In addition, in the near term, shale development causes labor and capital to be used that would otherwise be idle, again raising GDP. In the longer term, however, whether shale resources are available or not, the labor and capital available in the economy will be used at roughly their maximum sustainable rates, so the additional labor and capital used to produce shale resources or energy-intensive goods will mostly be drawn away from the production of other goods and services. As a result, there will be no net change in GDP through that last route, although GDP will continue to

be increased by shale development in the other ways just described.

On net, CBO estimates that real (inflation-adjusted) GDP will be about two-thirds of 1 percent higher in 2020 and about 1 percent higher in 2040 than it would have been without the development of shale resources. The actual effect on GDP could be higher or lower than that estimate, depending on the uncertain factors noted above—the abundance of shale resources, the fraction of those resources that will be recoverable, and the cost of developing that fraction—as well as on other considerations.

How Will Shale Development Affect the Federal Budget?
The increase in GDP resulting from shale development has increased federal tax revenues, and it will continue to do so. That increase will be slightly larger than the GDP increase in percentage terms, CBO expects. Specifically, CBO estimates that federal tax revenues will be about three-quarters of 1 percent (or about $35 billion) higher in 2020 and about 1 percent higher in 2040 than they would have been without shale development.

Shale production also contributes to federal receipts through payments that the developers of federally owned resources make to the government—but that contribution has been modest and will continue to be, because most shale resources are not on federal land. Working from EIA's projections of the future production of tight oil and shale gas, and also from its own forecasts of oil and natural gas prices, CBO estimates that federal royalties from shale (minus the amounts that the federal government transfers to the states) will be about $300 million annually by 2020.

What Policy Options Would Affect Shale Development?
There are a number of ways that the Congress could affect shale development and thus affect the oil and gas markets, economic output, and the federal budget. This report considers options that would change export policies—easing the current ban on exports of crude oil, repealing it, or changing the government's criteria for judging applications to export liquefied natural gas (LNG)—and concludes that the options would probably increase domestic production but have little effect on

Figure 1.

Hydraulic Fracturing and Horizontal Drilling

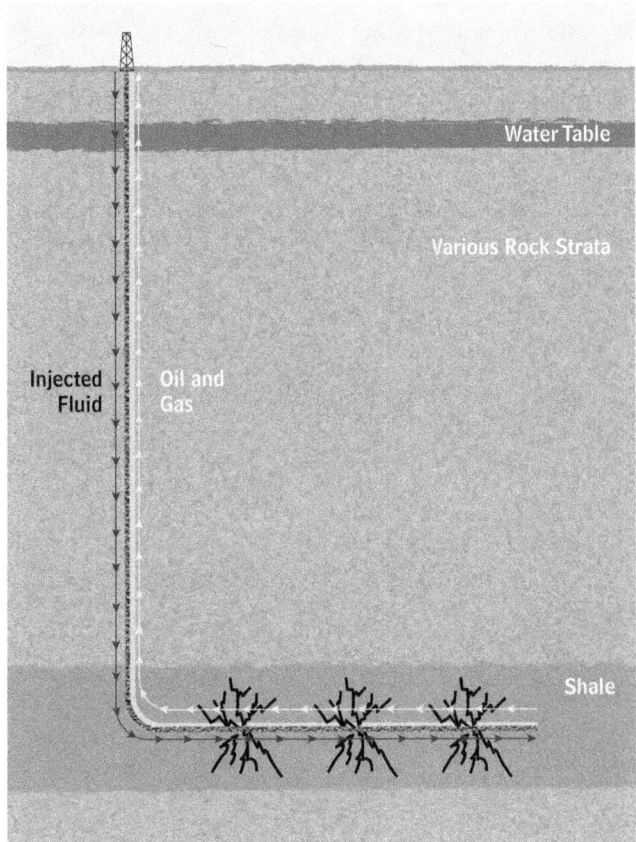

Source: Congressional Budget Office.

prices. That increase in production would probably make GDP and federal revenues slightly higher than they would be under current export policies.

Policy choices related to environmental regulation, such as whether the federal government should regulate further the environmental effects of shale development or leave such decisions to the states, are outlined in Appendix A. The Congress could also affect shale development through policies not considered here, such as those related to the infrastructure used to transport and process domestic shale gas and tight oil.

Hydraulic Fracturing and Shale Resources

Hydraulic fracturing, used with horizontal drilling and other advances in drilling technology, is a way to reach

and extract natural gas and oil locked in certain rock formations, especially shale formations.[4] Some forms of hydraulic fracturing have been used to extract fossil fuels since the 1950s, but the method was not successfully combined with horizontal drilling for another 30 to 40 years, and it began to have a substantial impact on natural gas and oil production only in the past decade.

The process (often called fracing or fracking) begins with drilling a vertical well to the depth of a shale formation and, from there, drilling a horizontal well into the formation, which is much wider than it is thick (see Figure 1). A high-pressure mixture of water, chemicals, and small particles is pumped into the well to create fractures in the formation. Those fractures are held open by the particles as the injected fluid is withdrawn. Oil and gas then flow from the fractures into the well and up to the surface.

According to EIA estimates, of the shale gas in the United States that is technically recoverable—that is, that could be developed with current technology—25 percent is in the Marcellus Shale formation, which is located mainly in New York, Pennsylvania, and West Virginia (see Figure 2). The formations with the next-largest quantities of shale gas are the Haynesville-Bossier Shale in Texas and Louisiana, containing an estimated 15 percent of technically recoverable resources; the Eagle Ford Shale in Texas, containing about 10 percent of those resources; and the Barnett Shale, also in Texas, and also containing about 10 percent of those resources.

The Eagle Ford and Austin Chalk Shales in Texas, which are found at different depths but underlie some of the same land, together account for about 40 percent of

---

4. This report focuses on shale development recently enabled by the use of hydraulic fracturing and horizontal drilling. It does not consider the use of those techniques to produce "tight gas" (that is, natural gas extracted from less dense geologic formations), because such development has occurred for many years, or to enhance production from conventional oil and gas supplies. Nor does it consider kerogen shale (also known as oil shale), another kind of rock from which oil can be produced, because the oil is not extracted with hydraulic fracturing and its generally high cost is expected to keep production low for the foreseeable future.

Figure 2.

Shale Formations in the United States

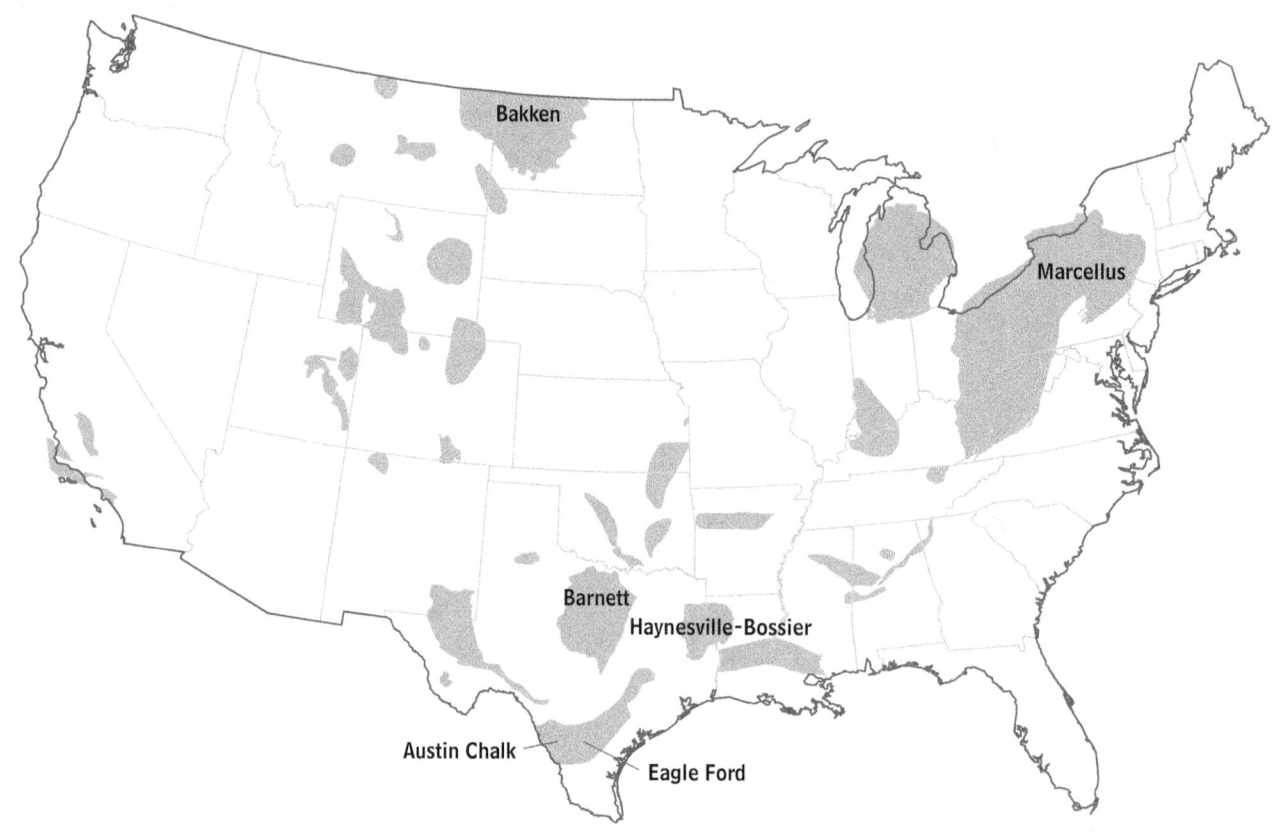

Bakken

Marcellus

Barnett

Haynesville-Bossier

Austin Chalk

Eagle Ford

Source: Congressional Budget Office based on data from the Energy Information Administration, "Detailed Oil and Gas Field Maps"
(accessed October 2, 2014), http://go.usa.gov/VKt4.

technically recoverable tight oil. An additional 20 percent
is in the Bakken Shale in North Dakota and Montana.[5]

---

5.   The percentages in these two paragraphs are based on the most
recently available data that distinguish shale gas from tight gas:
Energy Information Administration, U.S. Crude Oil and Natural
Gas Proved Reserves, 2012 (April 2014), Tables 2 and 4,
www.eia.gov/naturalgas/crudeoilreserves; Energy Information
Administration, *Assumptions to the Annual Energy Outlook 2013*
(May 2013), Table 9.3, http://go.usa.gov/vvne; and
Louis Sahagun, "U.S. Officials Cut Estimate of Recoverable
Monterey Shale Oil by 96%," *Los Angeles Times* (May 20, 2014),
http://tinyurl.com/pnknuct. More recent data do not distinguish
shale gas from tight gas, but they do show a notable development:
that the Spraberry/Wolfcamp Shale in Texas has become an
important source of technically recoverable tight oil. See Energy
Information Administration, *Assumptions to the Annual Energy
Outlook 2014* (June 2014), Table 9.3, http://go.usa.gov/sagw.

Effects on Energy Markets

The production of shale gas and tight oil has risen dramatically over the past decade. The shale gas increase has
been so large that, if it came from a separate country, that
country would now be the world's third-largest natural
gas supplier (behind first-place Russia and the U.S. supplies not from shale). Because of shale gas, domestic
production of all natural gas is on pace to increase for
the ninth straight year and has reached record highs
(see Figure 3). With that increase in production, the
wholesale price of natural gas in North America fell by
about 70 percent, in inflation-adjusted terms, between
2008 and 2012, reaching its lowest level since 1998

Figure 3.

Annual Production of Natural Gas in the United States

Trillions of Cubic Feet

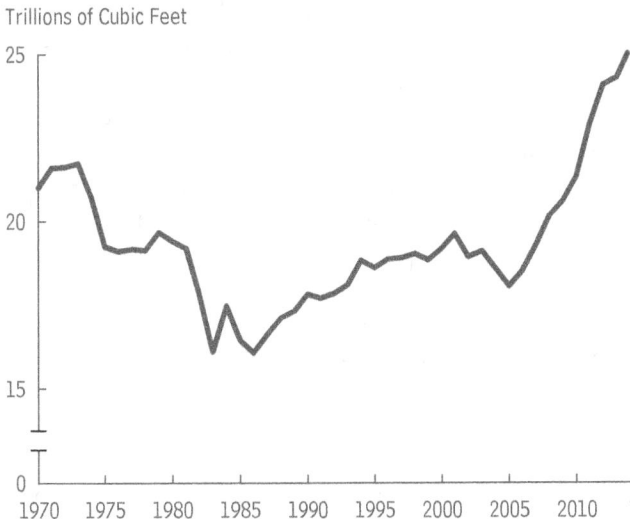

Source: Energy Information Administration, "U.S. Dry Natural Gas Production" (accessed November 14, 2014), http://go.usa.gov/7XgQ.

Note: Production in 2014 is an estimate based on monthly totals from January through September.

(see Figure 4).[6] Though gas prices rebounded somewhat in 2013 and 2014, they remain low compared with the recent historical record.

The production of crude oil in the United States has also boomed, with domestic output up for the fifth straight year because of tight oil. But the increase in tight oil production, unlike the corresponding increase in shale gas, has had only a modest impact on prices.[7] As this report discusses below, the increase in tight oil is small relative to domestic oil consumption, and oil prices, unlike gas prices, are determined in a global market.

Shale development has affected other energy markets as well; for example, it has reduced the demand for coal. As the production of shale gas and tight oil increases, its effects on other energy markets—such as those for coal, for nuclear and renewable energy, and for energy-conserving equipment—will also increase. In addition, some analysts predict that energy-intensive production activities will increasingly relocate to the United States to take advantage of low gas prices.

Trends in the Markets for Shale Gas and Tight Oil

According to EIA's projections, supply and demand conditions will keep the production of shale gas and tight oil growing in coming years—in fact, growing enough so that the overall domestic production of oil and gas will continue to grow, reversing the trend of the past several decades. Because of the growth in production, the domestic price of gas will be lower than it would have been in the absence of shale resources; so will the price of oil, though to a lesser extent. Those lower prices will boost oil and gas consumption and net exports of refined products and natural gas. (The quantity of exports will depend partly on federal policy choices, as the next section discusses.)

Production. EIA expects the production of shale gas to rise from 9.5 Tcf in 2013 to 20 Tcf in 2040. That increased production will be responsible for almost all the growth in overall U.S. gas supplies, which are projected to rise 13 Tcf over that time, from 24 Tcf in 2013 to 37 Tcf in 2040.

Also, EIA projects that the production of oil from shale formations will be 1.4 million barrels per day higher in 2020 than in 2013 but only 0.2 million barrels per day higher in 2040 than in 2013. That projection includes both tight oil and natural gas plant liquids, such as ethane, propane, and butane, which are sometimes obtained

---

6. Energy Information Administration, "Natural Gas Prices" (accessed November 4, 2014), http://go.usa.gov/Kfch. Retail prices paid by final buyers of natural gas have declined less sharply, because part of the retail price of natural gas covers the cost of gas transportation and taxes—costs that do not change as the wholesale price of gas declines. In addition, partly because of differences in the percentage of retail prices that cover the cost of transportation and taxes, not all buyers have seen the same declines in retail prices: The declines have been greatest (roughly 60 percent since 2008) for large buyers, such as industrial users and electricity producers, and smallest (about 25 percent) for residential customers.

7. Crude oil prices have declined by about a third in recent months, but not because of any sudden or dramatic increase in the availability of shale resources. Other factors, such as a rapid increase in Libyan production and a slowdown of consumption in Europe and Asia, have had a greater influence. A sustained reduction in crude oil prices would reduce U.S. production of both conventional oil and tight oil in the near term, but the degree to which the recent weakness in oil prices will persist is unclear. All else being equal, lower trajectories for the price of oil or the production of tight oil through 2020 or 2040 would reduce CBO's estimates of the economic and budgetary effects of tight oil in those years.

in the production of shale gas and are good substitutes for certain petroleum products. EIA expects that the production of tight oil alone will grow from 3.5 million barrels per day in 2013 to a peak of 4.8 million by about 2020; it will then fall back to 3.2 million by 2040, as production from existing wells wanes and new wells in less promising areas yield less oil. Natural gas plant liquids are projected to increase modestly but more steadily, from 2.5 million barrels per day in 2013 to 3 million in 2040.

Prices. The availability of shale energy (that is, shale gas and tight oil that come to the market) should lessen the growth of energy prices in the years ahead. Shale gas will probably have a larger impact in that way than tight oil will. One reason is simply that shale gas is more plentiful, relative to domestic consumption. Shale gas production today equals about 35 percent of total U.S. gas consumption, whereas tight oil production equals only about 15 percent of U.S. consumption of liquid fuels. By 2040, according to EIA's most recent long-term projection, shale gas will account for about 60 percent of all natural gas consumed in the United States, but tight oil will still represent only about 15 percent of all liquid fuels consumed.[8]

Another reason that U.S. natural gas markets will be more affected than domestic oil markets by shale energy is that they have far less international exposure. Natural gas markets are broadly split into three regions—North America, Europe, and Asia—and gas is transported within each of those regions by pipeline at relatively low cost. But the cost of transporting gas *between* regions is significant, primarily because it must undergo costly liquefaction before being shipped on oceangoing vessels. Therefore, little trade occurs between regions, and prices in the three markets are largely independent of one another. Crude oil, by contrast, can be moved around the world at relatively low cost by tanker ship or pipeline, which means that oil prices are approximately the same around the world. The effects of domestic shale gas production will therefore be concentrated in North America, whereas the effects of domestic tight oil production will be diffused internationally.[9]

Though shale energy is expected to lessen the growth of energy prices, continued growth in demand means that

those prices will nevertheless continue to rise. EIA currently projects a doubling of the real price of natural gas in North America by 2040, as well as a roughly 30 percent increase in the real price of oil worldwide. Prices would be still higher if the production of U.S. shale energy turned out to be lower than EIA expects. For example, according to a recent EIA analysis, if shale resources turned out to be only half as abundant as the agency projected in its baseline scenario, domestic prices in 2040 would be about 40 percent higher for gas and somewhat less than 3 percent higher for oil than they would be under the baseline scenario.[10] (Similarly, CBO estimates that if shale resources did not exist at all, the price effects would be roughly twice as large, with gas and oil prices in 2040 that were roughly 70 percent and 5 percent higher, respectively, than currently projected.)

Consumption and Net Exports. Because of the lower prices that will result from shale development, the domestic consumption of gas will be higher than it would have been in the absence of shale resources; net exports of natural gas (that is, international consumption of domestically produced gas) will also be higher. Of the expected 13 Tcf increase in natural gas production between 2013 and 2040, EIA projects that 53 percent (about 7 Tcf) will be reflected in greater net exports and 47 percent (about 6 Tcf) in increased domestic consumption (see Figure 5). Roughly 75 percent of that projected increase in domestic consumption will be in the electric power and industrial sectors.

The electric power sector's increased consumption of gas will result not only from that sector's higher overall production of electricity but also from the growing importance of gas relative to other fuels. The EIA projection shows that by 2040, natural gas's share of the total fuel used in the electric power sector will grow from 21 percent to 25 percent; renewable fuels' share will also grow,

---

8. Energy Information Administration, *Annual Energy Outlook 2014 With Projections to 2040*, DOE/EIA-0383(2014) (April 2014), http://go.usa.gov/8KyF (PDF, 12 MB).

9. For a broader discussion of geographic price differences in world energy markets, see Congressional Budget Office, *Energy Security in the United States* (May 2012), www.cbo.gov/publication/43012.

10. Energy Information Administration, *Annual Energy Outlook 2014 With Projections to 2040*, DOE/EIA-0383(2014) (April 2014), http://go.usa.gov/8KyF (PDF, 12 MB). The "low-resource" scenario includes reductions in tight gas resources as well as in tight oil and shale gas resources. Economically viable shale gas is much more plentiful than tight gas, however, and accounts for about four-fifths of the total 2040 difference in gas production between that scenario and EIA's baseline scenario.

Figure 4.

Average Annual Price of Natural Gas

2012 Dollars per Million British Thermal Units

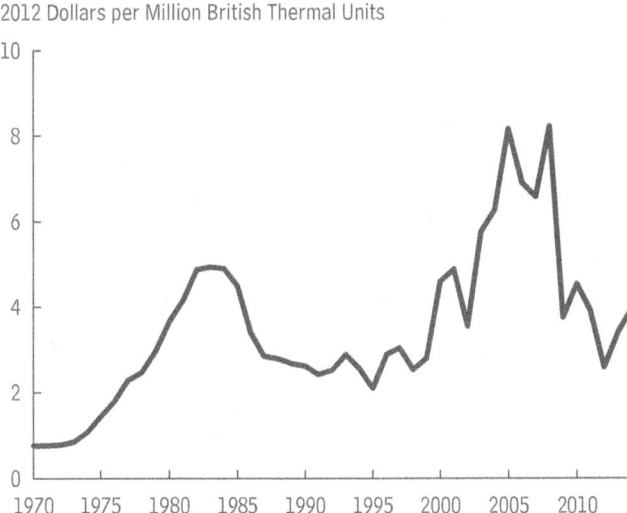

Source: Congressional Budget Office based on data from the Energy Information Administration, "U.S. Natural Gas Wellhead Price" (accessed November 4, 2014), http://go.usa.gov/7X2G, and "Henry Hub Natural Gas Spot Price" (accessed November 4, 2014), http://go.usa.gov/7X2z.

Note: Prices shown from 1970 through 2012 are average wellhead prices for gas produced nationally. Because the 2013 and 2014 averages are not available yet, averages for those years are derived from a historical relationship between average wellhead prices and the prices recorded at the Henry Hub natural gas pipeline interconnection in Louisiana. The Henry Hub price is commonly used as a benchmark for wholesale gas prices throughout North America. CBO converted prices into 2012 dollars by means of the GDP (gross domestic product) deflator.

while those of coal and nuclear power will shrink. In the industrial sector, by contrast, the increased use of natural gas is expected to be roughly in line with that sector's growth.

Unlike the consumption of natural gas, the consumption of liquid fuel will be slightly lower in 2040 than in 2013, decreasing by about 1 percent, EIA estimates. The main reason is that changes in driving habits and improvements in vehicles' fuel economy are expected to reduce U.S. demand for liquid fuels. Also, the use of natural gas in the transportation sector is expected to grow, further lowering demand for petroleum.

The United States is currently a net importer of natural gas and of liquid fuels; that is, it consumes more than it

produces (see Figure 6). But the production of shale resources has significantly reduced net imports—from nearly 4 Tcf of natural gas in 2007 to about 1.5 Tcf in 2013, and from 12.5 million barrels per day of liquid fuels in 2005 to 6.2 million in 2013. EIA projects that the United States will become a net exporter of natural gas in 2017 and remain so through 2040.[11] However, EIA expects the country to remain a net importer of liquid fuels throughout the projection period; net imports are projected to decline to about 5 million barrels per day as tight oil production increases, to stay steady for a few years, and then to return to current levels by 2040, as tight oil production falls.

Policy Options Related to Exports and Their Effects on Domestic Prices

To the extent that federal policy allows oil and gas to be imported and exported, their domestic prices reflect supply and demand not only in the United States but in other countries as well. Analysts and policymakers are currently proposing various changes to policies governing exports of crude oil and liquefied natural gas. In CBO's view, such changes would probably increase domestic oil and gas production, but they would probably have only a small effect on the domestic price of gas and a negligible effect on the domestic price of oil (which, again, is largely determined in the world market).

As this report discusses below, increases in oil and gas production resulting from shale development have boosted U.S. economic output and federal receipts and will continue to do so. The further increases in production that would result from the changes in export policies considered here would also have positive economic and budgetary effects, but smaller ones.

Exports of Crude Oil. Federal law prohibits the export of domestically produced crude oil, with few exceptions.[12] In 2013, only about 1 percent of crude oil produced in the United States (about 120,000 barrels per day) was

---

11. Ibid.

12. The President is authorized to approve exports of crude oil that are in the national interest. With a few exceptions, such approval takes the form of a license from the Commerce Department's Bureau of Industry and Security. That bureau's policy is to approve certain categories of export applications—the most important category being exports to Canada for consumption or use there—and to review other applications on a case-by-case basis.

Figure 5.

Natural Gas Production in the United States in 2013 and 2040

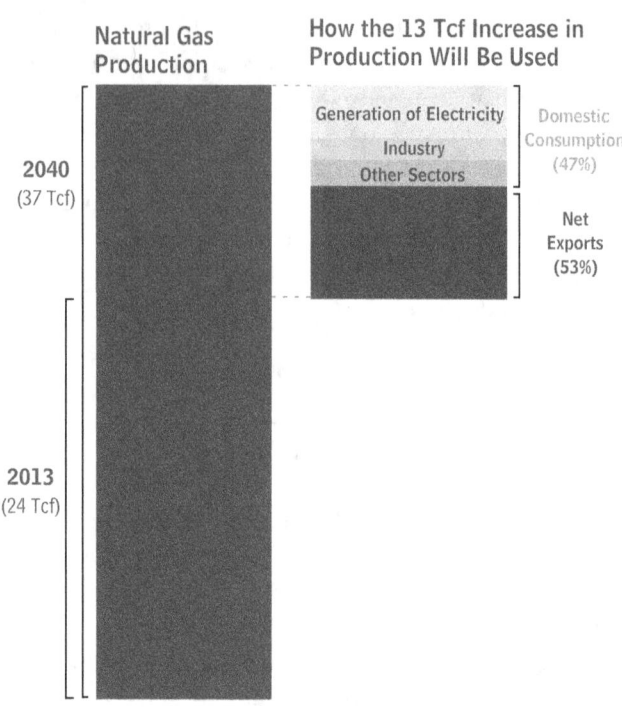

Source: Congressional Budget Office based on data from the Energy Information Administration, *Annual Energy Outlook 2014 With Projections to 2040*, DOE/EIA-0383(2014) (April 2014), http://go.usa.gov/8KyF (PDF, 12 MB).

Note: Tcf = trillion cubic feet.

exported, essentially all of it to Canada.[13] In contrast, federal policy does not restrict U.S. exports of refined petroleum products or of natural gas plant liquids, biofuels, and other nonpetroleum liquids. Together, exports of those fuels totaled 3.6 million barrels per day in 2013—a record high—with roughly half of that volume consisting of gasoline and diesel fuel.

Policy Options. Because U.S. supplies of crude oil have grown so dramatically in recent years, some policymakers have called for the ban on crude exports to be repealed. Current policy could also be changed less dramatically. For example, exports might be permitted not only to Canada but to certain other countries as well, such as Mexico, the countries of Central America, or all nations

with which the United States had free-trade agreements (FTAs). Alternatively, the volume of allowed exports could be capped, or exports could be restricted to particular grades of crude oil.

Potential Effects of Those Options. Outright repeal of the ban on crude exports would probably lower world prices of oil and of liquid fuels produced from oil, but only slightly, and changes that left some export prohibitions in place would lower world prices even less. The reason is that prices depend on the total worldwide supply of crude oil, and the increase in total supply would probably be much smaller than the increase in the volume of U.S. crude exports. One recent study, for example, estimated that if the ban was repealed, U.S. crude exports would increase by as much as 1.5 million barrels per day, but world supply would increase by no more than 200,000 barrels per day—less than one-quarter of one percent of the current total.[14] Two factors explain the difference. First, what contributes to the total worldwide supply of oil is not U.S. *exports* but U.S. *production*, which would rise much less than exports would. For instance, the study estimated that if the ban was repealed and crude exports rose by about 1.5 million barrels per day, U.S. oil production would rise by only about 500,000 barrels per day.[15] (Domestic consumption would not change much, however, because U.S. crude *imports* would be higher as well, as the next paragraph explains.) Second, the net increase in world production would be smaller even than the increase in U.S. production, because the U.S. increase would drive some competing high-cost supplies from the market.

Perhaps counterintuitively, U.S. consumers of gasoline, diesel fuel, and other oil products would probably benefit, along with domestic oil producers, if the ban was repealed; domestic refiners would be adversely affected,

---

13. Energy Information Administration, "Petroleum & Other Liquids—Exports by Destination" (accessed December 8, 2014), http://go.usa.gov/8Nvx.

14. ICF International, *The Impacts of U.S. Crude Oil Exports on Domestic Crude Production, GDP, Employment, Trade, and Consumer Costs* (submitted to the American Petroleum Institute, March 2014), http://tinyurl.com/nnr8hxg.

15. A more recent study yielded similar findings: In its baseline projections, lifting the ban on U.S. exports of crude oil raised those exports by no more than 1.8 million barrels per day and world crude oil production by no more than 300,000 barrels per day. See Robert Baron and others, *Economic Benefits of Lifting the Crude Oil Export Ban* (submitted by NERA Economic Consulting to the Brookings Institution, September 2014), www.nera.com/67_8673.htm.

Figure 6.

Consumption and Supply of Natural Gas and Liquid Fuels in the United States

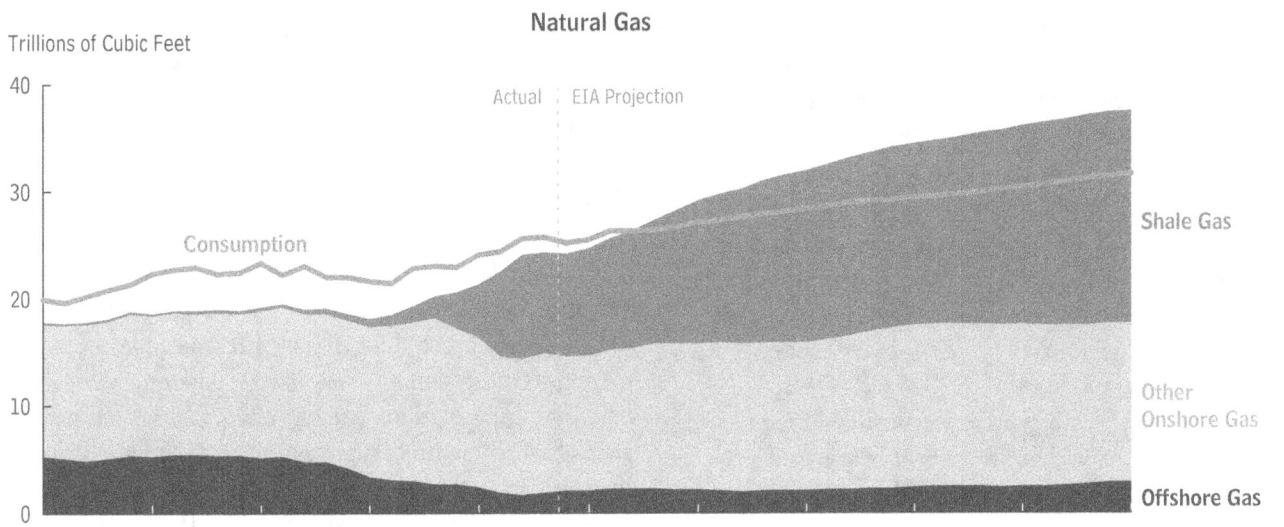

Natural Gas

Trillions of Cubic Feet

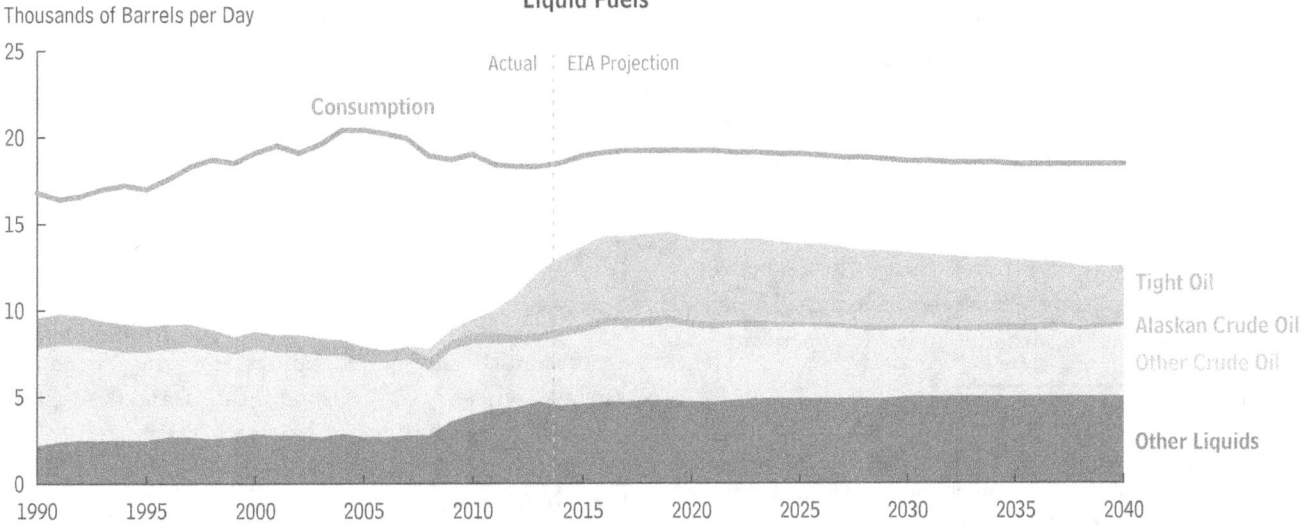

Liquid Fuels

Thousands of Barrels per Day

Source: Energy Information Administration, *Annual Energy Outlook 2014 With Projections to 2040*, DOE/EIA-0383(2014) (April 2014), http://go.usa.gov/8KyF (PDF, 12 MB).

Notes: Tight oil is crude oil extracted from shale and certain other dense rock formations by means of hydraulic fracturing. The category "Other Liquids" consists of natural gas liquids, biofuels, and processing gain (the additional barrels of petroleum produced by refining crude oil into heavier and lighter products).

EIA = Energy Information Administration.

as would foreign oil producers. Consumers would benefit from small reductions—5 to 10 cents per gallon, in the baseline scenario of a recent study—in the domestic prices of oil products, because those prices depend primarily on the world price of crude oil, which would decline slightly once lower-priced U.S. crudes were available in the international market.[16] By contrast, the prices of domestic light crude oils (which include tight oils) seen by some U.S. crude oil producers and petroleum refiners would rise. Refineries in the United States are better configured than refineries abroad to process heavy crudes, so under the current ban, light crudes are less valuable—and therefore sell for less—in the United States than in the global market.[17] If the ban was repealed, some domestic refiners would continue to buy light crudes, and others would increase their imports of heavy crudes; in either case, the cost of their crude oil inputs would be higher than it had been under the ban, and because they would continue to sell their refined products at levels closely linked to the world price of oil, their profits would fall.

Exports of Natural Gas. The United States trades significant quantities of natural gas with Canada and Mexico. Using pipelines, it currently exports about 1.6 Tcf per year to those two countries, and it imports about 2.9 Tcf per year, virtually all of it from Canada.[18] The pipelines through which gas travels between Canada, the United States, and Mexico create a unified North American

market in which the price of gas is determined by the total supply and demand of all three countries. Once the United States is a net pipeline exporter, as EIA projects it will be within a decade, domestic gas prices will be higher than they would be without pipeline exports.[19]

The only way to transport significant volumes of natural gas to countries that are not connected to the United States by gas pipelines is to liquefy the gas and move it by ship. The United States has very little capacity to do that, because it was expected until recently to be a substantial importer for decades to come.[20] But as hydraulic fracturing and related technologies have become widespread in the United States, natural gas has become much cheaper here than in foreign markets; in 2013, average gas prices were about three times higher in Europe and about four times higher in Japan, both of which are large gas consumers.[21] Such price differences, if they last, could make selling LNG overseas profitable, despite the significant cost of liquefying natural gas, transporting it, and converting it back into gaseous form.

Policy Options. Restrictions on gas trade by pipeline are not allowed under the free-trade agreements that the United States has with Canada and Mexico. Exports of LNG, however, are subject to restrictions under current law, which the Congress could modify in various ways.

Currently, the construction of facilities to liquefy and export natural gas requires approval from the Federal Energy Regulatory Commission (FERC), and the exports themselves must be approved by the Department of Energy (DOE). Prospective exporters can apply for blanket authority to ship LNG to countries in either or both of two groups: those with FTAs with the United States that cover natural gas and those without such agreements.

---

16. Ibid.

17. For example, for more than three years, the price of West Texas Intermediate (WTI)—a domestically produced light crude whose price is used as a benchmark for the prices of other U.S. crude oils—has been lower than the price of Brent, a North Sea oil that is broadly representative of other world crude supplies, despite the fact that WTI is higher-quality and usually slightly more expensive. Without the ban on U.S. crude exports, the relationship between those prices would more closely reflect the historical pattern, so that the price of WTI would rise relative to that of Brent.

18. Energy Information Administration, "U.S. Natural Gas Exports and Re-Exports by Country" (accessed November 4, 2014), http://go.usa.gov/NfKF, and "U.S. Natural Gas Imports by Country" (accessed November 4, 2014), http://go.usa.gov/Nf8B. A major reason that the United States both exports gas to Canada and imports gas from it is that some of the imports are reexported to Canada. Because it has limited pipeline infrastructure to move gas from its western regions, where most of its gas is produced, to its east, Canada serves its eastern demand by exporting gas to the western United States and importing it from the eastern United States.

19. The United States has not been a net pipeline exporter since the 1950s. By 2040, EIA expects pipeline exports to triple and imports to decline by 30 percent. See Energy Information Administration, *Annual Energy Outlook 2014 With Projections to 2040*, DOE/EIA-0383(2014) (April 2014), http://go.usa.gov/8KyF (PDF, 12 MB).

20. Only one LNG export facility is currently operating in the United States, and it is scheduled to export less than 0.1 Tcf of LNG over the next two years. See ConocoPhillips, "Kenai LNG Exports" (accessed August 25, 2014), http://tinyurl.com/o36tdo7.

21. World Bank, "World Bank Commodities Price Data (The Pink Sheet)" (December 2, 2014), http://tinyurl.com/qjbfqmf (PDF, 233 KB).

Exports to countries without FTAs, which account for roughly 80 percent of LNG imports worldwide, require DOE to determine that the exports would be in the public interest; DOE regards LNG exports to FTA countries as automatically being in the public interest.

As of October 2014, four LNG export terminals, proposed for Louisiana, Maryland, and Texas, had received approval for construction and for exports to countries without FTAs; if those terminals are built in the next several years, their combined capacity of about 2.5 Tcf will represent roughly 8 percent of North American gas consumption. Four more facilities, proposed for Florida, Louisiana, and Oregon and having a combined capacity of 1.5 Tcf, have recently been authorized by DOE to export LNG to countries without FTAs, but none of them have received approval for construction from FERC. All told, the roughly 30 applications that have sought full approval from FERC and DOE would create facilities that could export about 13 Tcf of LNG per year, an amount equal to roughly 40 percent of the natural gas consumed in North America.[22]

If the Congress wanted to change LNG export capacity, it could alter the criteria for DOE's approval of such exports to countries without FTAs. For example, it could require DOE to treat applications to export to those countries the same way that it treats applications to export to FTA countries—that is, automatically assuming that they are in the public interest. Such a change would speed the review process and make approvals more likely. Alternatively, the Congress could change the federal review process to make approvals of LNG exports less likely. For instance, when determining whether to allow LNG exports to a country without an FTA with the United States that covered natural gas, DOE could be required to give particular weight to the effects that the resulting higher domestic gas prices would have on low-income households in this country.

Potential Effects of Those Options. If the pending applications were approved, and export capacity of 13 Tcf per year was built and fully used, that 40 percent decline in supply in North America would boost gas prices considerably (unless suppliers greatly increased production in response to even a small price increase). But that much

capacity might be approved without being built or fully used, in which case the actual volume of LNG exports might be much smaller. Whether approval of facilities led to construction and use would depend heavily on whether the difference between North American and overseas gas prices remained large enough to justify the costs of producing and exporting LNG.

On the one hand, today's large price gap could narrow—for example, if some new LNG facilities began operating, increasing the supply of natural gas overseas and reducing its price there while raising it here. The price gap could also narrow if major foreign suppliers of natural gas increased production to protect their market share; if new overseas gas resources, particularly shale gas, came to market; or if North American demand grew faster than supply. On the other hand, the price gap could widen further in the future, giving domestic firms an even bigger incentive to export gas—if, for example, worldwide demand for gas remained high but little additional LNG liquefaction and export capacity was built outside North America, or if North American gas supplies grew faster than demand.

A 2012 study commissioned by DOE analyzed future gas prices in various scenarios with different supply and demand conditions and different amounts of available export capacity. Most of the scenarios showed a future gap between U.S. and international gas prices too small to create much overseas demand for U.S. LNG; exports in those scenarios were accordingly small or nonexistent, even if a large amount of export capacity was approved.[23] Those findings were broadly confirmed in a 2014 update of the study (not commissioned by DOE), which found that under expected supply and demand conditions, allowing 2 Tcf or more of export capacity would result in only a 2 percent to 5 percent increase in domestic gas prices.[24] However, in scenarios in which sizable export capacity was approved and fully used, domestic prices would rise more sharply. For example, the more recent study estimated that with exports of about 4 Tcf per

22. Department of Energy, "Summary of LNG Export Applications of the Lower 48 States" (accessed November 4, 2014), http://go.usa.gov/KfYj.

23. W. David Montgomery and others, *Macroeconomic Impacts of LNG Exports From the United States* (submitted by NERA Economic Consulting to the Department of Energy, December 2012), http://go.usa.gov/KfGd (PDF, 4 MB).

24. Robert Baron and others, *Updated Macroeconomic Impacts of LNG Exports From the United States* (submitted by NERA Economic Consulting to Cheniere Energy, Inc., March 2014), http://tinyurl.com/p5vcjl9.

year—an amount consistent with the capacity of projects already approved by DOE, including those awaiting approval from FERC—domestic natural gas prices would probably be about 15 percent higher than they would have been with no export capacity. It also estimated that with exports of about 13 Tcf per year—roughly the capacity of all LNG facilities that have been approved or are currently seeking approval—prices would be 30 percent to 45 percent higher. But to support such high exports, overseas demand for LNG from the United States or U.S. supplies of shale resources (or both) would have to be much higher than projected by EIA at the time the studies were conducted.

EIA's most recent projection, which CBO uses in its baseline scenario, has the United States exporting about 2 Tcf per year of LNG by 2020 and about 3.5 Tcf by 2040.[25] Taking into account differences in the economic conditions underlying EIA's projection and those underlying the studies discussed above, CBO estimates that the projected 3.5 Tcf of exports would increase domestic gas prices in 2040 by 10 percent or less, relative to the prices that would exist with no exports of LNG.[26]

To the extent that market conditions supported LNG exports, making capacity available to allow those exports would raise GDP—in part because more domestic gas would be produced, but also because the gas would be sold overseas at higher prices than at home. However, that increased GDP would not accrue to people in the United States uniformly. Higher prices for gas exported overseas would mean greater profits for U.S. gas producers; but the fact that domestic prices, too, would rise would mean that U.S. gas consumers faced higher costs. One of the studies mentioned above estimated that an increase in North American gas prices of $1 per million British thermal units, or Btus (about five times the increase found in the baseline scenario of the 2014 update to the DOE study), would increase costs for gas and electricity by $50 per year for U.S. households with

annual income less than $20,000 and by $90 per year for those with annual income above $100,000.[27] Some households—for example, those that owned shares of companies that produced gas, those that owned land in gas-rich areas, and those with members employed in the gas industry—would enjoy higher income that at least partly offset, if not outweighed, the increased gas and electricity costs.

Another effect of LNG exports would be to increase the integration of the North American gas market with the European and Asian markets. That would both increase the exposure of domestic consumers to supply shocks overseas and ameliorate the domestic effects of reductions in North American supplies. However, a full consideration of the effects of LNG exports on household income and market integration is beyond the scope of this report.[28]

Uncertainty in the Projections

Projections of shale development's impact on energy markets are inherently uncertain. A recent illustration of the uncertainty was EIA's energy market forecast in 2012, which projected that 2013 tight oil and shale gas production would total 0.9 million barrels per day and 7.6 Tcf, respectively.[29] The agency now expects 2013 production to have totaled 3.5 million barrels per day and 9.4 Tcf.[30]

25. Energy Information Administration, *Annual Energy Outlook 2014 With Projections to 2040*, DOE/EIA-0383(2014) (April 2014), http://go.usa.gov/8KyF (PDF, 12 MB).

26. CBO's calculation combined information from two sources: projections of future gas prices and production levels from EIA's *Annual Energy Outlook 2014 With Projections to 2040*; and estimates of the price sensitivity of gas production and of the relationship between gas production and LNG exports from Robert Baron and others, *Updated Macroeconomic Impacts of LNG Exports From the United States*.

27. Michael Levi, *A Strategy for U.S. Natural Gas Exports*, Discussion Paper 2012-04 (Brookings Institution, June 2012), http://tinyurl.com/nsxo7zo. The study's estimates were based on EIA's Residential Energy Consumption Survey for 2005, the latest information available at the time. Using data now available for 2009 does not materially affect those average costs. See Energy Information Administration, "Residential Energy Consumption Survey" (2009), Table CE2.1, http://go.usa.gov/8Kvz (XLS, 52 KB).

28. Other policy considerations not discussed here include the effects of extending the benefits of trade in natural gas to countries that do not agree to certain provisions that generally accompany free-trade agreements (such as safer conditions for workers and environmental protection) and the possibility that some actions that the United States might take to constrain LNG exports could prompt international challenges under the rules of the World Trade Organization.

29. Energy Information Administration, *Annual Energy Outlook 2012 With Projections to 2035*, DOE/EIA-0383(2012) (June 2012), http://go.usa.gov/7dhz.

30. Energy Information Administration, *Annual Energy Outlook 2014 With Projections to 2040*, DOE/EIA-0383(2014) (April 2014), http://go.usa.gov/8KyF (PDF, 12 MB).

There are many reasons for the uncertainty. Some involve the future availability of shale resources and others the future demand for those resources. Uncertainty also exists about the factors that have affected recent gas prices, and those factors influence estimates of future prices.

The Availability of Shale Resources. The main reason for the difficulty of projecting the market effects of shale development, CBO believes, is uncertainty about the future availability of shale resources. To estimate future availability, analysts must assess three items, each of which is itself uncertain:

- The total quantity of shale resources in the ground;

- The quantity of technically recoverable resources at various points in the future, which is the fraction of total resources that could be recovered at each of those points with the technology then available; and

- The costs of developing those technically recoverable resources (which are relevant to future availability because developers would not extract resources that could be developed only at an exorbitant cost).

What makes the first two items uncertain is clear: Not all shale resources have been identified, and improvements in technology are difficult to predict. In 2011, for example, the U.S. Geological Survey (USGS) released an estimate of technically recoverable shale gas from the Marcellus Shale that, because hydraulic fracturing and horizontal drilling had made more resources recoverable, was about 40 times larger than its previous estimate, which was issued in 2003.[31] However, in its annual estimates, EIA had expected even greater growth, so it lowered its estimate of the shale gas present in the Marcellus by about 65 percent after considering the USGS finding.[32] Similarly, on the basis of production trends and a revised understanding of the area's geology, EIA recently lowered its estimate of technically recoverable tight oil reserves in California's Monterey Shale formation by 96 percent.[33]

The third item, the cost of developing technically recoverable resources, is uncertain for many reasons. One is that limited information exists about the rate at which tight oil and shale gas wells become less productive over time. Initial evidence suggests that production declines much more rapidly for tight oil and shale gas wells than for conventional oil and gas wells; some estimates suggest that it falls 80 percent or more over the first three years of operation. However, because shale wells have not been in operation very long, it is difficult to draw firm conclusions about their lifetime rates of production. If the productivity of tight oil and shale gas wells turns out to decline more slowly than experts project, current estimates will have overstated the cost of producing a given quantity of shale energy from a given quantity of resources. The reverse will be the case if productivity declines more quickly than expected.

Another reason that production costs are uncertain is that limited information is available about the distribution of well productivity. A recent analysis found that the amount of shale gas that new wells in the same rock formation yielded in the first few months was distributed very unevenly, with high production from relatively few wells and low production from the rest.[34] As production diminishes in the areas that were developed first because they were considered the most promising, and as development moves into other areas, the percentage of wells that are highly productive may fall, raising the cost of finding such wells and thus the average cost of developing shale resources. Alternatively, if exploration methods improve, the percentage of wells that are highly productive may increase.

The Demand for Shale Energy. Domestic and foreign demand for shale energy depends on many uncertain factors, such as population growth, economic growth, the cost of conventional oil and gas, the cost of other competing energy sources, and the energy intensity of the economy (that is, the average amount of energy used in

31. James L. Coleman and others, *Assessment of Undiscovered Oil and Gas Resources of the Devonian Marcellus Shale of the Appalachian Basin Province, 2011*, FS 2011-3092 (U.S. Geological Survey, August 2011), http://pubs.usgs.gov/fs/2011/3092/.

32. Energy Information Administration, *Annual Energy Outlook 2012 With Projections to 2035*, DOE/EIA-0383(2012) (June 2012), http://go.usa.gov/7dhz.

33. Louis Sahagun, "U.S. Officials Cut Estimate of Recoverable Monterey Shale Oil by 96%," *Los Angeles Times* (May 20, 2014), http://tinyurl.com/pnknuct.

34. J. David Hughes, *Drill, Baby, Drill: Can Unconventional Fuels Usher in a New Era of Energy Abundance?* (Post Carbon Institute, February 2013), www.postcarbon.org/drill-baby-drill/.

producing a dollar's worth of GDP).[35] None of those factors can be forecast with precision. For instance, driving habits in the future, the supply of conventional oil and gas, and the cost of generating electricity from renewable fuels might differ from what is currently expected. Projections of foreign demand are subject to additional uncertainty about transportation costs, other costs of trade, and foreign governments' trade policies.

The Factors Influencing Recent Gas Prices. Still another source of uncertainty in estimates of the effects of shale development involves the extent to which the recent declines in gas prices reflect factors other than the increased availability of shale gas. At least three such factors may be at work. First, the recent recession and slow economic recovery have reduced gas prices by reducing demand. Second, producers may be supplying more gas than they would have otherwise, given current prices, because of the boom in gas development that occurred in the second half of the last decade, when gas prices were much higher. Third, gas production is being supported by oil prices, which have been fairly high until recently. Gas producers in areas rich in natural gas plant liquids—which, as this report noted earlier, are sometimes obtained in the production of shale gas and are good substitutes for certain petroleum products—have been willing to produce and sell natural gas at a loss so that they can obtain those liquids, the prices of which are more closely linked to the price of crude oil than to the price of natural gas.[36]

The more those three factors (or others) have been responsible for today's low gas prices, the smaller a role has been played by the current availability of shale gas, and the more estimates may overstate the future sensitivity of gas prices to the availability of shale gas.

---

35. Consumers who want to purchase gas or oil do not specifically demand shale gas or tight oil. Here, "demand for shale energy" at a given price refers to the excess of demand for the fuel at that price above the amount of the fuel supplied from conventional resources.

36. Researchers recently concluded that a highly productive gas well in the Barnett Shale required a price of about $3 per million British thermal units (mmBtu) of gas to generate a 10 percent rate of return in the absence of natural gas plant liquids, but only about 50 cents per mmBtu if such liquids were present. See Peter Behr, "Barnett Shale Has Surprisingly More to Give, Texas Researchers Find," *EnergyWire* (September 25, 2013), www.eenews.net/energywire/stories/1059987786.

Suppose, for instance, that more of the decline in gas prices since 2008 resulted from the economic slowdown than a particular model accounts for, and that less resulted from the growth of shale gas availability. In that case, the model would have overestimated the past effects of shale gas availability on prices, and projections based on that model would similarly overestimate the future effects of shale gas availability on prices.

Effects on Economic Output

In the long run, CBO estimates, the development of shale resources will lead to higher GDP by increasing the productivity of existing labor and capital and by increasing the amount of labor and capital in use. Specifically, CBO projects that real GDP will be 0.7 percent higher in 2020 and 0.9 percent higher in 2040 than it would have been without shale development.

In recent years, shale development has probably had a larger effect on GDP, having employed labor and capital that would otherwise have been unused because of weak demand for goods and services. That larger effect will probably persist over the next few years—that is, as long as interest rates remain low and output remains distinctly below its maximum sustainable level. But after output moves back toward its maximum sustainable level, labor and capital used to produce shale resources or gas-intensive goods will mostly be drawn away from the production of other goods and services, which means that shale development will have a smaller net effect on GDP.

In the Next Few Years

Shale development has boosted GDP in recent years and will continue to do so. However, CBO has not quantified the effect over the next few years, because shale development's short-term effects on the economy, other than on the output of oil and gas, are especially difficult to measure. Those effects include increased investment in the oil and gas industry and in industries that support it; increased investment and production in other industries because energy prices are lower than they would otherwise be; and increased demand for goods and services because of greater household income—all of which increase GDP. Shale development also reduces the amount of labor and capital available for other uses and reduces the production of energy from conventional resources; those effects reduce GDP.

Increased Output of Oil and Gas. Shale development has increased U.S. output of tight oil and shale gas, raising GDP. The market value of shale gas produced in 2013 (reflecting the contributions of both the gas industry and the other industries that supply goods and services used to produce shale gas) was about $35 billion. In the same year, the market value of tight oil, including natural gas plant liquids produced by hydraulic fracturing, was about $160 billion. Combined, sales of shale gas and tight oil therefore totaled about $195 billion, or roughly 1.2 percent of GDP.

Increased Investment in the Oil and Gas Industry and in Supporting Industries. Shale development has probably raised GDP in recent years through greater spending on the development of new wells. Between 2004 and 2012, investment in the oil and gas extraction industry increased from 0.4 percent of GDP to 0.9 percent.[37] However, that increase included investment in conventional oil production that probably would have occurred even without shale development because of the sharp rise in oil prices over that period. CBO did not estimate how much of the increase in investment could be attributed to shale development.

In addition, industries that support the oil and gas sector have spent more on new facilities and equipment, such as pipelines and trains, as a result of shale development. CBO did not quantify that increase in investment either.

Increased Investment and Production in Other Industries. Industries that use natural gas intensively—such as the steel, petrochemical, fertilizer, and electricity industries—have expanded production to take advantage of energy prices that are lower than they would have been without shale development. Such industries have become more competitive internationally because of the fall in energy prices in the United States: A number of new U.S. petrochemical and fertilizer facilities are being planned, for example, and one company is in the process of moving two methanol plants from Chile to Louisiana.[38] Thus, shale development has boosted GDP by raising investment in, and production from, energy-intensive

industries—but it is very difficult to estimate the magnitude of that effect.[39]

Increased Demand. Higher employment resulting from shale development, along with a larger capital stock resulting from increased investment in the development and use of shale resources, has led to higher household income and thus greater demand for goods and services. Some of that increased demand has been met by the additional production from the energy-intensive industries described above. However, much of the increase has been for products supplied by firms that do not directly benefit from lower natural gas and oil prices. In order to meet the increased demand, those firms have increased employment and investment, which has raised GDP still further in the short term.

Less Labor and Capital Available for Other Uses. The effects described above have shifted some workers and capital away from other uses, which means that some economic activity has been forgone. That forgone output has partly offset shale development's positive effects on GDP. Although CBO has not quantified the forgone output, the fact that the economy's slow recovery from the recent recession has left many resources underused suggests that the amount is small.

Less Production From and Investment in Conventional Energy Resources. As shale development has made energy prices lower than they would have been otherwise, the production of gas and oil from some conventional supplies has become unprofitable and has therefore been abandoned, and some investment in conventional sources of gas and oil has not been undertaken. Similarly, electric utilities' substitution of natural gas for coal has reduced production from and investment in coal mining. The forgone production and investment, like the reduced output from sectors that lost labor and capital, has partly offset shale development's positive effects on GDP. CBO

---

37. CBO calculated that increase with data from the Bureau of Economic Analysis, "Fixed Assets Accounts Tables," Table 3.7ESI (accessed September 20, 2014), http://go.usa.gov/vwCC.

38. Methanex Corporation, *Annual Report 2013* (Methanex, March 2014), http://tinyurl.com/lwhxkma (PDF, 601 KB).

39. According to one report, the effect of hydraulic fracturing on investment by energy-intensive industries has been small so far but could grow in the future; see Jan Hatzius and others, *Is the Economy Gaining "Fracktion?"* US Economics Analyst 13/42 (Goldman Sachs, October 2013). Another has found that the fall in the price of natural gas since 2006 is associated with a 2 percent to 3 percent increase in activity for the entire manufacturing sector; see William R. Melick, *The Energy Boom and Manufacturing in the United States*, International Finance Discussion Papers 1108 (Board of Governors of the Federal Reserve System, June 2014), http://go.usa.gov/vvDW (PDF, 672 KB).

estimates that conventional gas production falls by about one-tenth the amount of an increase in shale gas production, which means that the resulting loss in GDP in 2013 was probably small.[40] The effect of reduced investment in conventional energy on GDP in 2013 is harder to quantify.

In the Longer Term

Shale development will raise GDP in the longer term in two ways: increasing the productivity of existing labor and capital, and increasing the amount of labor and capital in use. CBO estimates that, as a result, real GDP will be 0.7 percent higher in 2020 and 0.9 percent higher in 2040 than it would have been without shale development, although those estimates are subject to considerable uncertainty.[41] The longer-term effects of shale development on GDP will probably be smaller than the near-term effects described above (see Box 1).

Increased Productivity. Shale development raises GDP by increasing the productivity of labor and capital. That increased productivity is projected to make GDP 0.4 percent higher in 2020 and 0.5 percent higher in 2040 than it would have been in the absence of shale development.

Some of the increased productivity comes from the labor and capital used in shale development itself, which are more productive because of hydraulic fracturing and horizontal drilling than they would have been without those techniques. CBO estimates that the value of the tight oil and shale gas produced in both 2020 and 2040 will be about 1.3 percent of real GDP. But in the absence of hydraulic fracturing and horizontal drilling, CBO

estimates, the labor and capital now projected to be used to produce that output would contribute only about 1.0 percent to GDP in 2020 and about 0.9 percent in 2040. The boost to GDP from reallocating labor and capital into the production of tight oil and shale gas is the difference between those estimates: about 0.3 percent of GDP in 2020 and 0.4 percent in 2040. (For details about that estimate and others in this section of the report, see Appendix B.)

Another component of the increased productivity resulting from shale development comes from replacing high-cost conventional oil and gas with shale resources. Because less labor and capital are now required to produce the same amount of oil and gas, the shift frees up labor and capital, which are used to produce other goods, thereby increasing GDP. However, because the reduction in conventional oil and gas will be modest, the resulting increase in GDP will be small in both 2020 and 2040.

The rest of the increased productivity comes from labor and capital that are used more efficiently elsewhere in the economy because of increased consumption of oil and gas. As energy-intensive products and methods of production grow cheaper, the same amount of output can be produced with less labor and capital. For example, as the cost of generating electricity from gas has fallen, some electric utilities have increased their productivity by switching from coal to gas. Through such shifts, GDP will be about 0.1 percent higher in both 2020 and 2040 than it would have been without shale development, CBO estimates.

Higher output would also result if shale development led manufacturing to become a larger share of the economy and if labor was generally more productive in manufacturing than in other sectors. However, recent earnings data do not demonstrate that labor productivity is higher in manufacturing. Although the average weekly earnings of employees in manufacturing were higher than those of all private-sector employees in 2013, hourly earnings were about the same, meaning that most of the difference in weekly earnings was due to a longer average workweek in manufacturing.

Increased Total Labor and Capital. Shale development will also raise GDP by increasing the amounts of labor and capital used in the economy, in CBO's assessment. That increase will happen in at least two ways. First, the increase in output generated by higher productivity that

---

40. That CBO estimate is based on Energy Information Administration, *Annual Energy Outlook 2014 With Projections to 2040*, DOE/EIA-0383(2014) (April 2014), http://go.usa.gov/8KyF (PDF, 12 MB).

41. Those estimates assume no restrictions on exports of LNG in 2020 and beyond. If the difference between domestic and overseas gas prices increased demand for U.S. exports of LNG, but those exports were constrained because federal permits had not been issued, the increases in GDP would be lower. Such a constraint would keep domestic LNG prices lower than they would be otherwise, which would benefit domestic businesses and households that used gas; however, those benefits would not fully offset the loss to gas producers. See W. David Montgomery and others, *Macroeconomic Impacts of LNG Exports From the United States* (submitted by NERA Economic Consulting to the Department of Energy, December 2012), http://go.usa.gov/KfGd (PDF, 4 MB).

Box 1.
Why the Economic Effects of Shale Development Will Be Larger in the Near Term

The positive effects of shale development on gross domestic product (GDP) are partly offset by output that is forgone when labor and capital are shifted away from other uses. That offsetting effect has not been large so far, in the Congressional Budget Office's assessment, because the economy's slow recovery from the recent recession has left many resources unused. However, the effect will be larger once the economy moves back toward producing its maximum sustainable level of output. At that point, the labor and capital shifted into the production of shale resources or energy-intensive goods and services will mostly be drawn away from the production of other goods and services. Consequently, shale development's net effect on GDP is likely to be smaller in the longer term than in the near term.

The redistribution of labor and capital will occur in various ways. For example, some higher-cost production of natural gas from conventional resources will become unprofitable, pushing labor and capital elsewhere. The composition of domestic production will shift toward energy-intensive manufacturing and away from other industries. And increased net exports of natural gas and oil will boost the value of the dollar, making goods produced in the United States more expensive relative to U.S. imports and therefore leading to reduced production of those

goods. (Economists refer to that phenomenon as Dutch disease, remembering the discovery in 1959 of the Groningen gas field in the Netherlands, which led to large exports of natural gas and a surge in the value of the Dutch currency in the late 1960s and early 1970s—and thereby made Dutch manufacturing less competitive.) The increase in the value of the dollar will probably be small, but it will affect all U.S. exports and imports and would probably have a discernible effect on the economy.

A recent study illustrates the difference between shale development's effects on GDP in the near term and in the longer term. An average of the conservative and optimistic scenarios in the study indicates that shale resources are expected to boost maximum sustainable GDP by 0.65 percent and actual GDP by 1.35 percent between 2013 and 2020. The difference between those estimates illustrates the additional response of GDP to shale development when the economy is not operating at its maximum sustainable level of output.[1]

---

1. See Trevor Houser and Shashank Mohan, *Fueling Up: The Economic Implications of America's Oil and Gas Boom* (Peterson Institute for International Economics, 2014), Chapter 4, http://bookstore.piie.com/book-store/6567.html.

---

was described above will result in additional income; part of that income will be saved and then invested, increasing the capital stock. Second, the higher productivity will increase wages, improving the return to workers from each hour of work and encouraging them to work more. Because of those effects, CBO estimates, GDP will be 0.3 percent higher in 2020 and about 0.4 percent higher in 2040 than it would have been without shale development.[42]

Other effects of shale development on the total amounts of labor and capital (and in turn on GDP) are highly uncertain, so CBO did not estimate them. For example, if the industries that produce and use natural gas and oil, or those that supply infrastructure for shale development,

are more capital-intensive than those that see production fall as a result of shale development, the demand for capital and thus the overall return on investment in the United States will be higher. That higher rate of return will lead to increases in private saving and in capital inflows from abroad. But under the same circumstances, companies' desire to replace labor with capital will reduce the return to working, reducing the labor supply.

Other Considerations. Two more considerations should be mentioned that are related to shale development's effects on the economy in the longer term. One involves a reduction in the dollar cost of U.S. imports; the other involves uncertainty in the estimates of economic effects.

The Cost of Imports. Shale development confers an economic benefit that raises the standard of living in the United States but does not show up as greater GDP. Specifically, increased net exports of natural gas and oil boost the value of the dollar, making imports cheaper and allowing consumers to buy more and businesses to invest more for a given quantity of exports and a given amount of GDP. CBO has not quantified that effect, however.

Uncertainty. CBO's estimates of shale development's effects on GDP are accompanied by significant uncertainty of various kinds. The estimates rest on baseline projections of the prices of shale gas and tight oil, of the quantities of those fuels produced in the United States, and of the profitability of that production—and as is explained earlier (in the section "Uncertainty in the Projections"), all of those projections are uncertain, because of underlying uncertainty about demand for natural gas and oil, demand for other forms of energy, the availability of shale resources, and exploration and production technology.

CBO therefore estimated the effects of shale development not only according to those baseline projections but also under two alternative scenarios. In the first scenario, prices, production, and profitability are all lower than projected in the baseline. Prices of natural gas and oil (reflecting recent EIA projections of price uncertainty) are about 25 percent lower in 2015 than they are in the baseline projection, then grow more slowly than they do

in the baseline, and are about 50 percent lower by 2040. The production of shale gas and tight oil is about 40 percent lower than in the baseline by 2040, a figure that is consistent with what EIA calls its low-resource scenario. And the average cost of producing shale gas rises 75 percent as quickly as the price of natural gas, compared with 50 percent as quickly in CBO's baseline projection.[43]

In the second alternative scenario, the three factors are all *higher* than projected in the baseline. The prices of natural gas and oil start out about 35 percent higher than they are in CBO's baseline projection and grow to be roughly 50 percent higher.[44] The production of shale gas and tight oil is about 40 percent higher than in the baseline by 2040; and profitability is higher because the average cost of producing shale gas rises only 25 percent as fast as the price of natural gas.

In the first scenario, shale development makes real GDP 0.4 percent higher in 2020 and 0.3 percent higher in 2040 than it would have been otherwise. (The effect is smaller in 2040 because the economy then will be larger relative to the market value of shale energy in the scenario.) In the second scenario, GDP is 1.3 percent higher in 2020 and nearly 2 percent higher in 2040 because of shale development.

Effects on the Federal Budget

The development of shale resources affects two kinds of federal receipts. The first, federal tax revenues, rise as shale development boosts GDP. The second, payments to the government by private developers of federally owned resources, also increase with shale development—but not much, because most of the nation's shale gas and tight oil is not owned by the federal government.

---

42. Some researchers have estimated that shale resources will have a much larger impact on the total amount of labor and capital used in the economy in 2020, resulting in a much larger impact on GDP. For example, one report estimates that shale energy could add a net 1.7 million permanent jobs by 2020 and boost GDP by 2 percent to 4 percent; see Susan Lund and others, *Game Changers: Five Opportunities for US Growth and Renewal* (McKinsey & Company, July 2013), http://tinyurl.com/mazev4d. Another report estimates that new energy supply may create 2.7 million to 3.6 million jobs by 2020, on net, and boost GDP by 2 percent to 3 percent; see Edward L. Morse and others, *Energy 2020: North America, the New Middle East?* (Citigroup, March 2012), http://tinyurl.com/mo7k7dt. Those researchers' estimates of net jobs created are much higher than CBO's. The difference probably arises because the other researchers think that labor supply responds more strongly to increases in wages; that in 2020, the economy will still not be producing its maximum sustainable level of output (so underused labor could still be drawn into shale development without reducing the labor available to other industries); or both. For a detailed discussion of CBO's estimating approach, see Appendix B.

43. That average cost will rise because more costly resources will be profitable to develop as natural gas prices rise. The projection that it will rise more slowly than natural gas prices is consistent with EIA projections that shale gas will continue to grow as a share of overall U.S. gas production.

44. The larger initial departure from baseline prices—35 percent, compared with 25 percent in the first scenario—is consistent with EIA's recent price forecasts, which in turn reflect market expectations (shown in futures prices and trading prices for options contracts) that near-term prices have more potential to be higher than expected than to be lower than expected. See Energy Information Administration, *Short-Term Energy Outlook* (November 2014), www.eia.gov/forecasts/steo/outlook.cfm.

Tax Revenues

The development of shale resources has increased economic activity in recent years and will continue to do so, as the previous section explains. That increased activity is reflected in higher income of various kinds, such as wages and salaries, income from partnerships and sole proprietorships, dividends, and corporate profits. And because that higher income is subject to a combination of individual income taxes, corporate income taxes, and payroll taxes, shale development increases federal tax revenues as well.

CBO expects the effect of shale development on revenues to be slightly higher in percentage terms than the effect on GDP. As the previous section also mentions, CBO estimates that real GDP will be 0.7 percent higher in 2020 and 0.9 percent higher in 2040 than it would have been without shale development. On the basis of that increase in GDP, CBO estimates that revenues will be higher by 0.8 percent (or about $35 billion) in 2020 and by 1.0 percent in 2040 than they would have been without shale development.[45]

In arriving at those rough estimates for 2020 and 2040, CBO assumed that the net effect of shale development on GDP would be allocated among the various types of taxable and nontaxable income, and across households in different tax brackets, in the same proportions in which overall GDP was expected to be allocated. Because the United States has a progressive individual income tax system—that is, one in which income in higher brackets is taxed at higher rates—that assumption led to the conclusion that shale development would have a greater effect on revenues than on GDP, in percentage terms. (By contrast, if the GDP added by shale development was unusually concentrated among people in the lowest tax bracket, shale development might have a smaller percentage impact on revenues than on GDP.)

Payments for Federally Owned Resources

The federal government receives payments from private developers of federally owned oil and gas. In the case of onshore oil and gas, about 90 percent of the payments are royalties on production; the rest are payments to obtain leases and rent on leases not yet put into production. All of the payments go initially to the U.S. Treasury, but under current law, the federal government generally pays about half to the states from which the resources were extracted. After adjusting for those payments to states, CBO estimates that net federal royalties from all onshore oil and gas leases will average about $1.4 billion a year over the 2015–2024 period.[46]

The portion of those royalties attributable to tight oil and shale gas production is uncertain because the government does not supply data breaking down production from federal lands by geologic formation. However, on the basis of information from state agencies and EIA, CBO estimates that in 2012, shale gas probably accounted for about 3 percent of onshore natural gas produced from federal land and tight oil for about 25 percent of onshore oil produced from federal land. Those estimates accord with the observation that few of the country's current and potential sources of shale gas and tight oil lie beneath federally owned land (see Figure 7).[47] For example, the Rocky Mountain region, which accounts for almost all of the natural gas (including shale gas) produced on federal land, is a minor source of the nation's supply of shale gas, yielding less than 1 percent of the total through 2024, according to EIA's projections.

---

45. Congressional Budget Office, *Updated Budget Projections: 2014 to 2024* (April 2014), www.cbo.gov/publication/45229, and *The 2014 Long-Term Budget Outlook* (July 2014), www.cbo.gov/publication/45471.

46. That figure is based on Congressional Budget Office, *An Update to the Budget and Economic Outlook: 2014 to 2024* (August 2014), www.cbo.gov/publication/45653. The 2015–2024 period is CBO's standard 10-year projection period.

47. Energy Information Administration, *Annual Energy Outlook 2012 With Projections to 2035*, DOE/EIA-0383(2012) (June 2012), p. 57, http://go.usa.gov/7dhz; David W. Houseknecht and others, *Assessment of Potential Oil and Gas Resources in Source Rocks of the Alaska North Slope, 2012*, FS-2012-3013 (U.S. Geological Survey, February 2012), http://pubs.usgs.gov/fs/2012/3013/; and David W. Houseknecht, *Assessment of Potential Oil and Gas Resources in Source Rocks (Shale) of the Alaska North Slope 2012—Overview of Geology and Results* (U.S. Geological Survey, 2012), pp. 5, 7–9, http://go.usa.gov/KfeH (PDF, 4 MB).

Figure 7.

Shale Formations and Federal Land in the United States

Current Sources of Shale Energy (▨) and Overlapping Federal Land (▰)

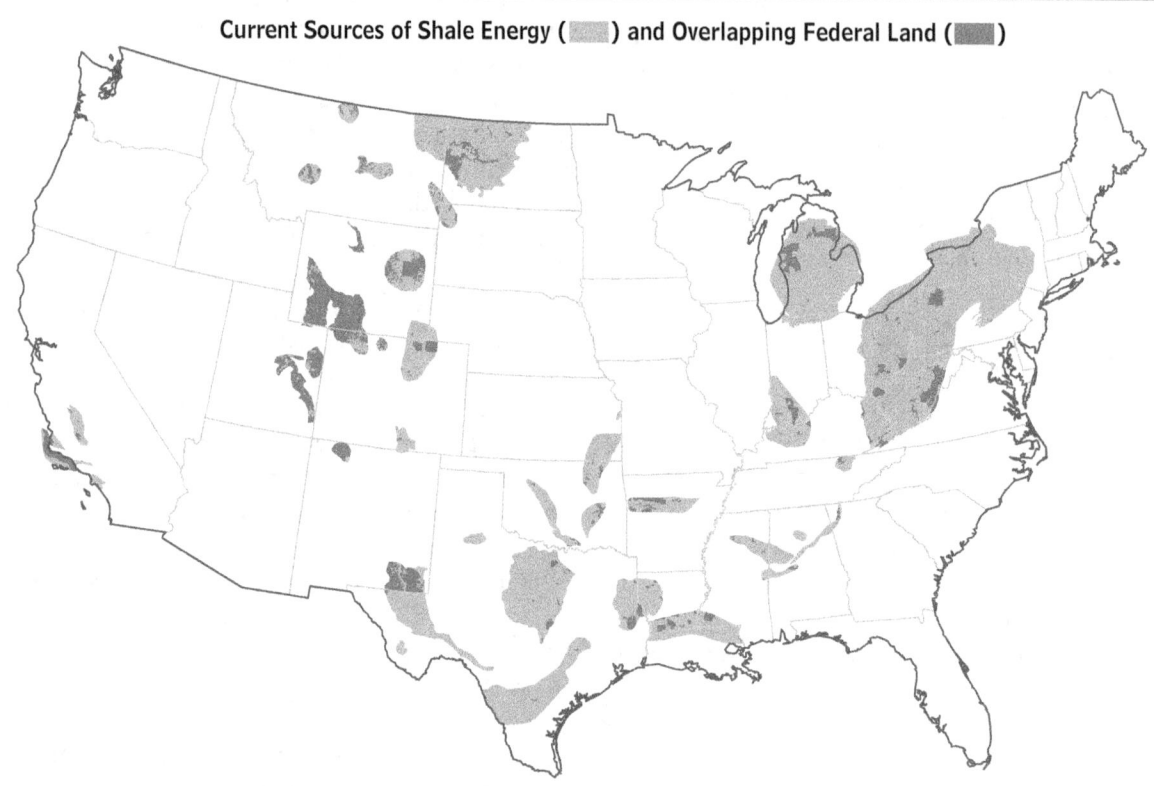

Potential Sources of Shale Energy (▨) and Overlapping Federal Land (▰)

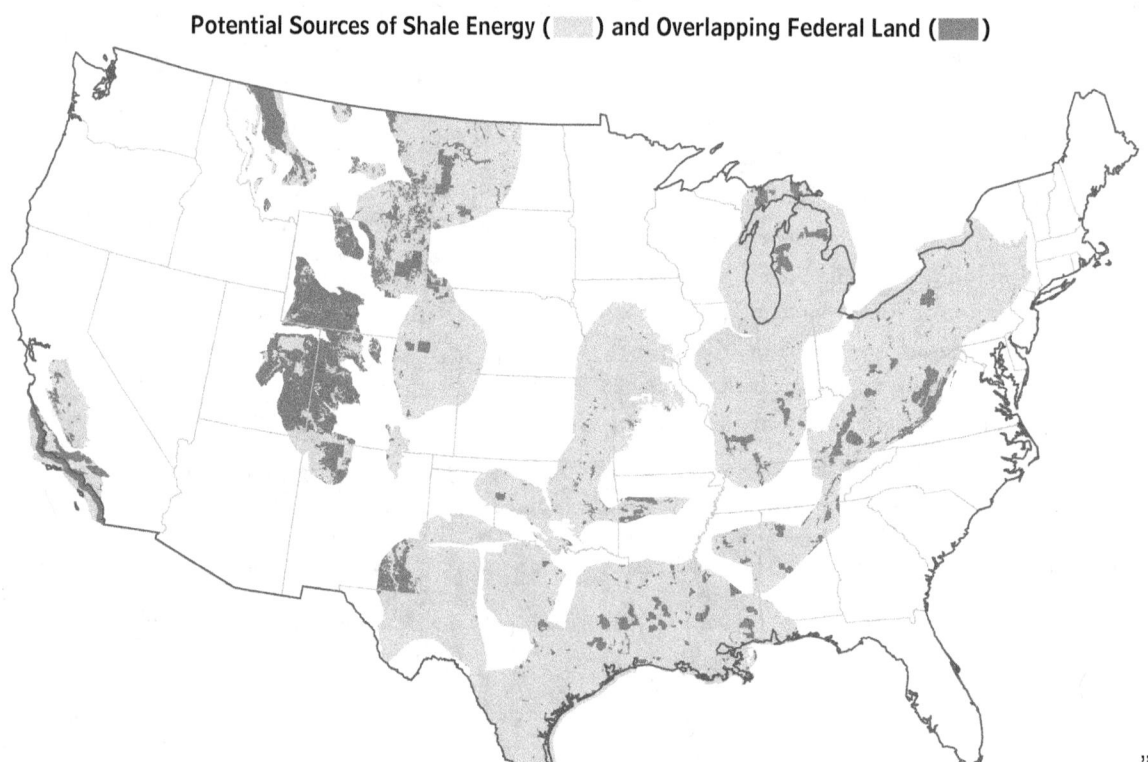

Source   "
    (accessed October 2, 2014), http://go.usa.gov/VKt4, and from the U.S. Geological Survey, "Federal Lands of the United States"
    (accessed October 2, 2014), http://go.usa.gov/vdzT.

Note: Shale energy is oil and natural gas extracted from shale and certain other dense rock formations by means of hydraulic fracturing.

In addition, the production of shale energy reduces the value of natural gas produced from federal *offshore* leases. That reduction diminishes the royalties (which are based on sales value) paid by the developers of those resources, and it therefore also diminishes the net effects of shale development on federal receipts.

On the basis of the preceding estimates and CBO's current forecast of oil and gas prices, along with EIA's projections of domestic production, CBO estimates that net federal royalties from tight oil and shale gas will total about $300 million a year by 2024. CBO anticipates that most of those royalties will come from the production of tight oil in the southeastern corner of New Mexico and in the Rocky Mountain region.[48] As with other estimates in this report, the $300 million figure is subject to substantial uncertainty.[49]

---

48. Total royalties from those regions will be higher because of the production of tight gas, which is not addressed in this report.

49. Various proposals have been made over the years for the federal government to increase the royalties that it receives by expanding access to energy resources on federally owned land. For more information, see Congressional Budget Office, *Potential Budgetary Effects of Immediately Opening Most Federal Lands to Oil and Gas Leasing* (August 2012), www.cbo.gov/publication/43527.

Effects on the Environment

Various observers are concerned that the development of shale resources may reduce the availability of water for other uses or contaminate it. They also have concerns, as well as hopes, about the effects of shale production on greenhouse gas emissions. The Congressional Budget Office (CBO) has not attempted to predict the future environmental consequences of shale development: The data about those consequences so far are not comprehensive enough, future consequences could differ from past ones because of the increasing scale of shale development, and future technological and regulatory developments are unclear. Instead, this appendix discusses the environmental effects of shale development on the basis of research and experience to date.[1] It also examines whether the federal government or state or local governments would be more likely to make economically efficient decisions about managing those effects.

Water Availability

Because hydraulic fracturing typically requires large quantities of water, shale development can contribute to strains on freshwater supplies. To date, conflicts between shale development and other uses of water have not been widespread, but some local ones have occurred.[2] In April and July of 2012, for example, after the flow volumes of local streams dropped below predetermined levels because of below-normal precipitation, the Susquehanna River Basin Commission temporarily suspended some

arrangements for water withdrawals, most of which were related to shale development. Such conflicts may intensify as shale development increases. One study estimates that freshwater withdrawals by the oil and gas industry in Texas's Haynesville-Bossier Shale will reach more than 3 billion gallons annually between 2020 and 2035—which is more than double the 2010 amount and corresponds to about 6 percent of total current water use in the area.[3]

Shale developers can reduce the amount of freshwater that they require by reusing it. However, the potential for reusing water at a particular site depends on how much flows back from the well, the cost of treating it so that it can be reused, and the freshwater sources and disposal options available in the area. For example, in the Marcellus Shale, where underground disposal wells for used water are scarce, some operations reuse nearly all of the water that flows back from their wells—but doing so reduces their freshwater needs by 30 percent at most, because much of the water that is pumped into the

---

1. The environmental effects discussed here are those that are associated particularly with shale development; effects that involve oil or gas more generally, such as leaks from pipelines, are not discussed. Concerns about local air pollution are also not discussed, because potential policies to address those concerns are similar to potential policies to address greenhouse gas emissions, which are discussed below.

2. Agriculture and thermoelectric power generation each account for about 40 percent of freshwater withdrawals nationwide; the rest is used by residences, businesses, and industry (including shale development). See Molly A. Maupin and others, *Estimated Use of Water in the United States in 2010*, Circular 1405 (U.S. Geological Survey, November 2014), http://pubs.usgs.gov/circ/1405/.

3. Texas Water Development Board, "Historical Water Use Estimates," county table for 2010 (accessed January 2014), http://go.usa.gov/KftG; Jean-Philippe Nicot and others, *Oil and Gas Water Use in Texas: Update to the 2011 Mining Water Use Report* (prepared by the Bureau of Economic Geology, University of Texas at Austin, for the Texas Oil and Gas Association, September 2012), http://go.usa.gov/KfzC (PDF, 3 MB); and Jean-Philippe Nicot, Bureau of Economic Geology, University of Texas at Austin, personal communication (January 8, 2014).

ground remains there.[4] Replacing freshwater in hydraulic fracturing with treated, nonpotable water or hydrocarbon-based fluids could also reduce demands on freshwater resources, but it is too soon to know whether such technological developments will prove widely effective and cost-competitive.

In general, rights to use freshwater are controlled by states and are more limited than typical property rights, so water is not bought and sold in a free market.[5] For example, some state laws prevent those whose use returns water to the local environment from selling their water rights to those whose use does not do so. During water shortages, other state laws may subject all holders of water rights to proportional reductions in use; alternatively, more recent holders may be required to reduce their use so that those who preceded them in obtaining rights to the same source of water can claim their full allocation. Because of such limitations, the amount of water that shale operations use may be smaller than the amount that would maximize the benefit of such water use to society. On the other hand, shale operations may have access to more water than the most socially beneficial amount if their impact on the environment is not appropriately regulated or reflected in market prices (say, by charges that cover wastewater treatment costs and other environmental impacts).

Water Quality

Concerns about the effect of shale development on water quality involve various sources of potential contamination: sediment from the construction of drilling platforms; drilling fluids; various chemicals, which constitute up to 2 percent of the fracturing fluid injected into a well; the liquid removed from a well, which can include not only the fracturing fluid but also material from the shale

formation (such as saltwater, organic compounds, heavy metals, and radioactive substances); and the extracted shale resources themselves.

Some of those contaminants might affect surface water, some might affect groundwater, and some might affect both (see Table A-1). However, certain routes of potential contamination—inadequate cleaning of the liquid removed from a fractured well before wastewater treatment facilities discharge it to surface water, for example, or underground migration from disposal wells to groundwater—are less likely than others, in part because they are regulated under the federal Clean Water Act of 1972 (CWA) or the federal Safe Drinking Water Act of 1974 (SDWA). In some cases, routes of potential contamination not currently regulated by the federal government could be addressed by regulations promulgated under state and local laws, especially those governing oil and gas production; in other cases, they already are, with varying degrees of stringency.[6]

Other provisions of the SDWA focus not on blocking contamination routes but on setting maximum concentrations of certain contaminants in water distributed by public drinking-water systems. Those provisions do not currently cover any of the 59 fracturing-fluid additives that companies have disclosed using routinely; however, limits for three of them—acetaldehyde, ethylene glycol, and methanol—are under consideration by the Environmental Protection Agency (EPA).[7] The SDWA concentration limits do not apply to private wells of drinking water, which serve about 15 percent of the U.S. population.

---

4. See Brian D. Lutz, Aurana N. Lewis, and Martin W. Doyle, "Generation, Transport, and Disposal of Wastewater Associated With Marcellus Shale Gas Development," *Water Resources Research*, vol. 49, no. 2 (February 2013), pp. 647–656, http://tinyurl.com/o9moyxc; and Matthew E. Mantell, "Deep Shale Natural Gas and Water Use, Part Two: Abundant, Affordable, and Still Water Efficient" (paper presented at the 2010 Ground Water Protection Council Annual Forum, Pittsburgh, Pa., September 27–29, 2010), p. 9, http://tinyurl.com/qxk2djc (PDF, 877 KB).

5. The federal government does have some influence on water allocations. See Congressional Budget Office, *How Federal Policies Affect the Allocation of Water* (August 2006), www.cbo.gov/publication/18035.

6. See Nathan Richardson and others, *The State of State Shale Gas Regulation* (Resources for the Future, June 2013), http://tinyurl.com/kwbt7l4 (PDF, 5 MB).

7. FracFocus, "What Chemicals Are Used" (accessed December 4, 2014), http://tinyurl.com/44m94y2; Environmental Protection Agency, "Drinking Water Contaminants" (accessed December 4, 2014), http://water.epa.gov/drink/contaminants/index.cfm; and Environmental Protection Agency, "Contaminant Candidate List 3" (accessed December 4, 2014), http://go.usa.gov/KG3m. The existing limits do cover four chemicals (benzene, ethylbenzene, toluene, and xylene) that are less commonly present in fracturing fluid but that may be present in fracturing fluid containing diesel, which is used at perhaps 2 percent of wells; see Mike Soraghan, "Hydraulic Fracturing: Diesel Still Used to 'Frack' Wells, FracFocus Data Show," *EnergyWire* (August 17, 2012), http://tinyurl.com/puduv5m.

Of course, regulations may not be effective in meeting their stated goals, or they may meet their goals but at excessive cost. Thus, an important question to ask about the regulations related to shale development is whether they have positive net benefits—that is, benefits (which depend partly on the extent of compliance) minus costs (which include enforcement costs). A second important question is whether those net benefits could be increased by making the regulations more or less stringent. A third is whether the regulations reflect adequate scientific understanding of the risks associated with the larger-scale shale development anticipated for the future. At the request of the Congress, the EPA is writing a report on the potential effects of hydraulic fracturing on resources of drinking water; it should provide information relevant to those questions.[8]

Greenhouse Gas Emissions

Some observers are hopeful that shale development will result in lower overall greenhouse gas emissions because burning natural gas releases less carbon dioxide, a greenhouse gas, than burning other fossil fuels does. Specifically, when measured per unit of energy output, carbon dioxide emissions from natural gas combustion are about 45 percent lower than from coal combustion and about 30 percent lower than from oil combustion.[9] However, the effect on greenhouse gas emissions of replacing coal or oil with shale gas depends not simply on the fuels' different emissions during combustion but also on their different emissions during extraction, transport, processing, and distribution.[10] Moreover, shale gas that does not displace coal or oil almost certainly increases total emissions unless technology is used to control the emissions. And emissions from all fossil fuels may increase as shale

development raises gross domestic product and increases the demand for energy.

Natural gas can more easily substitute for coal than for oil, because both gas and coal are commonly used to generate electricity. In fact, gas has been replacing coal in electricity generation for decades; that trend is expected to continue, partly because of the lower gas prices resulting from shale development. In contrast, there is little current potential for natural gas to replace oil, whether as transportation fuel or for heating: Few vehicles run on natural gas, and only about 10 percent of heating is fueled by oil (some of which, moreover, occurs in areas where gas lines do not exist).[11]

The effects on greenhouse gas emissions of substituting shale gas for coal are difficult to estimate. A key factor is emissions of methane, the primary component of natural gas, during the initial phases of shale gas extraction. Methane is a more powerful greenhouse gas than carbon dioxide; the latest report of the Intergovernmental Panel on Climate Change estimates that methane's impact on the climate, per unit of mass, is 84 times greater than carbon dioxide's over a period of 20 years and 28 times greater over 100 years.[12] The quantity of methane emissions depends critically on how producers handle the gas that emerges as the fracturing fluid injected into a well returns to the surface before the main extraction of shale energy. They might release it into the atmosphere; burn it off to reduce its climate impact, a process called flaring; or capture it with "green completion" technologies, which reduce total emissions by 90 to 95 percent and are the most effective way to minimize their impact on the

8. When the report is published, it will be available at www2.epa.gov/hfstudy.

9. Energy Information Administration, "Voluntary Reporting of Greenhouse Gases Program Fuel Emission Coefficients" (January 31, 2011), Table 1, www.eia.gov/oiaf/1605/coefficients.html.

10. For an overview of the measurement of emissions from natural gas systems, see A. R. Brandt and others, "Methane Leaks From North American Natural Gas Systems," *Science*, vol. 343, no. 6172 (February 14, 2014), pp. 733–735, http://tinyurl.com/lfbaay6.

11. Congressional Budget Office, *Energy Security in the United States* (May 2012), www.cbo.gov/publication/43012.

12. See Intergovernmental Panel on Climate Change, *Climate Change 2014: Synthesis Report* (IPCC, 2014), p. 100, Box 3.2, Table 1, http://www.ipcc.ch/report/ar5/syr/. The impact of methane in the short term is of concern because near-term global warming may trigger a rapid, nonlinear shift from one climate state to another without the possibility of reversal; for example, see Dave Levitan, "Quick-Change Planet: Do Global Climate Tipping Points Exist?" *Scientific American* (March 25, 2013), http://tinyurl.com/kbf247y.

Table A-1.

Possible Routes of Water Contamination by Shale Development

Contamination Route	Applicable Federal or State Regulation	Additional Information
Surface Water		
Sediment transported by storm water	Such contamination is regulated by CWA, but only if it violates a water quality standard; it is also regulated by some states.[a]	
Spills, overflows, and seepage from storage pits and tanks	CWA requires oil and gas producers to have plans to prevent and contain certain spills; in some cases, it requires discharge permits and pollution prevention plans.[b]	Some spills have occurred because of equipment failures that developers, viewing them as unlikely, had not addressed in their prevention plans.
Inadequate cleaning of flowback water—which consists of fracturing fluid and fluid from the rock formation that surface after hydraulic fracturing—by wastewater treatment facilities	Commercial and industrial sources of wastewater that would pose problems for wastewater treatment facilities are required by general standards in CWA regulations to pretreat their wastewater. Specific CWA standards for the pretreatment of flowback water from shale gas wells are expected to be proposed.[c] Some states also regulate the discharge of flowback water to wastewater treatment facilities.	Shale operations may not fully comply with pretreatment requirements. For example, CWA violations in the Allegheny River watershed between 2007 and 2011 were associated with wastewater from the Marcellus Shale processed at three Pennsylvania wastewater treatment plants between 2007 and 2011. Since mid-2011, because of a combination of state prohibitions and voluntary actions, shale operators have generally not sent flowback to Pennsylvania wastewater facilities that cannot provide pretreatment. Outside the Marcellus Shale area, underground disposal wells are more widely available, and developers therefore have less economic incentive to dispose of flowback water through wastewater treatment plants.
Groundwater		
Spills	CWA regulations designed to protect surface water may also protect groundwater.[d]	
Underground migration from rock formations targeted by developers	SDWA regulations apply to hydraulic fracturing only in the cases (about 2 percent of the total) in which the fracturing fluid includes diesel.[e]	Typically, the target formation is separated from sources of groundwater used for consumption by thousands of feet of rock.[f] Some exceptions may exist: A preliminary Environmental Protection Agency report found that some hydraulic fracturing operations in Wyoming that occurred less than 500 feet below depths reached by drinking-water wells may have contaminated deeper portions of the groundwater aquifer that the wells drew from.[g]

Continued

Table A-1.   Continued

Possible Routes of Water Contamination by Shale Development

Contamination Route	Applicable Federal or State Regulation	Additional Information
Groundwater (Continued)		
Underground migration from leaking wells	The federal government does not regulate well integrity; some states do.	Methane contamination of some drinking-water wells in Pennsylvania and Texas has been linked to leakage from hydraulically fractured shale gas wells.[h] Also, in 2011, Pennsylvania's Department of Environmental Protection fined a shale gas developer for contaminating well water. Water may contain methane for reasons unrelated to hydraulic fracturing, so it can be difficult to assign responsibility unless water samples were taken before shale development began.
Underground migration from disposal wells	Disposal wells require an SDWA permit.[i]	SDWA permits are issued after the government has determined that the rock formation where a disposal well will be located is sufficiently isolated from groundwater.

Source: Congressional Budget Office.

Note: CWA = Clean Water Act; SDWA = Safe Drinking Water Act.

a.   Sec. 303 of the Clean Water Act of 1972, Public Law 92-500 (codified at 33 U.S.C. §1313 (2012)).

b.   Sections 301, 311, 402, and 404 of the Clean Water Act, P.L. 92-500 (codified at 33 U.S.C. §§1311, 1321, 1342, and 1344 (2012)); 40 C.F.R. §117 (2013).

c.   Clean Water Act; 40 C.F.R. §437 (2013); and Notice of Final 2010 Effluent Guidelines Program Plan, 76 Fed. Reg. 66302 (October 26, 2011).

d.   Sec. 340 of the Clean Water Act, P.L. 92-500 (codified at 33 U.S.C. §1314 (2012)).

e.   Sec. 1421 of the Safe Drinking Water Act of 1974, P.L. 93-523 (codified at 42 U.S.C. §300h(d) (2012)); and Mike Soraghan, "Hydraulic Fracturing: Diesel Still Used to 'Frack' Wells, FracFocus Data Show," *EnergyWire* (August 17, 2012), http://tinyurl.com/puduv5m.

f.   See George E. King, "Hydraulic Fracturing 101" (paper presented at the Society of Petroleum Engineers Hydraulic Fracturing Technology Conference, The Woodlands, Texas, February 6–8, 2012), http://tinyurl.com/nt3r3w7 (PDF, 7 MB); Stephen G. Osborn and others, "Methane Contamination of Drinking Water Accompanying Gas-Well Drilling and Hydraulic Fracturing," *Proceedings of the National Academy of Sciences*, vol. 108, no. 20 (May 17, 2011), pp. 8172–8176, http://tinyurl.com/5w227nj; and Nathaniel R. Warner and others, "Geochemical Evidence for Possible Natural Migration of Marcellus Formation Brine to Shallow Aquifers in Pennsylvania," *Proceedings of the National Academy of Sciences*, vol. 109, no. 30 (July 24, 2012), pp. 11961–11966, http://tinyurl.com/ckfheor.

g.   Dominic C. DiGiulio and others, *Investigation of Ground Water Contamination Near Pavillion, Wyoming*, EPA 600/R-00-000 (draft, Environmental Protection Agency, December 2011), http://go.usa.gov/KGNG (PDF, 15 MB). "Less than 500 feet" is a CBO conversion from metric data on page xi of the report.

h.   Thomas H. Darrah and others, "Noble Gases Identify the Mechanisms of Fugitive Gas Contamination in Drinking-Water Wells Overlying the Marcellus and Barnett Shales," *Proceedings of the National Academy of Sciences*, vol. 111, no. 39 (September 13, 2014), pp. 14076–14081, www.pnas.org/content/111/39/14076.

i.   Safe Drinking Water Act; 40 C.F.R. §144.31 (2013).

climate.[13] The relative use of those three options is not well documented, and estimates vary widely.[14] In October 2012, the federal government began requiring shale gas developers either to use green completions or to flare their emissions.[15] By January 2015, green completions will be required for new hydraulic fracturing at gas wells, although a few categories of wells, such as those used to look for gas rather than to extract it, will still be allowed to flare.[16] There are no such requirements for oil wells.

Because of differences in production methods, shale gas that substitutes not for coal or oil but for gas from other sources increases total emissions of greenhouse gases when emission controls are not in place during the drilling and extraction phases.[17] Subsequent production activities, such as transport, processing, and distribution, may be even more significant sources of methane emissions,

but they are essentially the same for shale gas and conventional gas.[18]

A given volume of shale gas increases greenhouse gas emissions even more when it substitutes for energy sources other than fossil fuels—such as nuclear plants, windmills, and solar panels—because those energy sources emit no greenhouse gases at all in use. (A comprehensive comparison of those energy sources with shale gas would include the emissions associated with the construction of facilities, energy production, processing, and transport.) Similarly, when shale gas does not displace other energy sources but simply increases total energy use, all of the emissions resulting from its production, distribution, and use are net additions. All things being equal, such an increase in energy use would be the likely result of lower prices for natural gas and other forms of energy. For instance, families might choose to keep their homes warmer in the winter because the cost was lower; for the same reason, firms might reduce their investments in energy-efficient technologies. Also, the faster economic growth spurred by cheaper energy would increase demand for energy in general, including fossil fuels.

Environmental Policy in a Federal System of Government

There are a number of ways in which the government may influence the environmental effects of shale development: choosing standards for water use, water quality, and greenhouse gas emissions; deciding on the acceptable methods of meeting those standards; and funding related research. Federal policymakers may wish to consider whether the current division of regulatory responsibilities among federal, state, and local governments is likely to lead to decisions that maximize the net benefits to society.[19]

---

13. Environmental Protection Agency, "Summary of Requirements for Processes and Equipment at Natural Gas Well Sites" (accessed December 4, 2014), http://go.usa.gov/KGYe (PDF, 412 KB), and *Proposed New Source Performance Standards and Amendments to the National Emissions Standards for Hazardous Air Pollutants for the Oil and Natural Gas Industry* (July 2011), pp. 3–6, http://go.usa.gov/KGgH (PDF, 2 MB).

14. For instance, one 2012 assessment assumed that on a national basis, 70 percent of the methane emissions associated with extraction were captured, 15 percent were flared, and 15 percent were released into the atmosphere. The Environmental Protection Agency, by contrast, assumed that half of those emissions were flared and half released. See Francis O'Sullivan and Sergey Paltsev, "Shale Gas Production: Potential Versus Actual Greenhouse Gas Emissions," *Environmental Research Letters*, vol. 7, no. 4 (November 26, 2012), http://iopscience.iop.org/1748-9326/7/4/044030/; and Environmental Protection Agency, *Inventory of U.S. Greenhouse Gas Emissions and Sinks: 1990–2011*, 430-R-13-001 (April 2013), pp. 3-61 and 3-62, http://go.usa.gov/KGTT (12 MB).

15. The requirements, issued under the authority of the Clean Air Act, targeted emissions not of greenhouse gases but of volatile organic compounds and toxic air pollutants.

16. A recent study of the methane emissions from 27 hydraulically fractured wells of companies that voluntarily participated in the study found that two-thirds of the wells—generally, those with the largest potential methane emissions—captured or controlled methane produced during the initial phases of extraction, probably in part because of the new and emerging regulatory requirements. The remaining one-third released methane into the atmosphere, but those wells had much lower emissions potential, on average. See David T. Allen and others, "Measurements of Methane Emissions at Natural Gas Production Sites in the United States," *Proceedings of the National Academy of Sciences*, vol. 110, no. 44 (October 29, 2013), pp.17768–17773, www.pnas.org/content/early/2013/09/10/1304880110.

17. National Energy Technology Laboratory, *Environmental Impacts of Unconventional Natural Gas Development and Production*, DOE/NETL-2014/1651 (May 2014), pp. 39–56, http://go.usa.gov/vvXh (PDF, 3.1 MB).

18. See Francis O'Sullivan and Sergey Paltsev, "Shale Gas Production: Potential Versus Actual Greenhouse Gas Emissions," *Environmental Research Letters*, vol. 7, no. 4 (November 26, 2012), http://tinyurl.com/l2r8tcn.

19. For more on environmental policy in a federal system of government, see Congressional Budget Office, *Federalism and Environmental Protection: Case Studies for Drinking Water and Ground-Level Ozone* (November 1997), www.cbo.gov/publication/10546.

Standards

There is a stronger rationale for states and localities to set environmental standards for shale development if the costs and benefits of controlling the environmental effects of such development occur solely within their borders. The effects of shale development on the availability of water for other uses may be limited to a local area (which would not necessarily be a single local jurisdiction), or they may extend to a broader region—for instance, by affecting groundwater levels in regional aquifers. Similarly, the effects of shale development on water quality may be confined to a local area or extend beyond state boundaries. Rising or falling greenhouse gas emissions have global effects.

Other considerations include which level of government has the most information about underlying costs and benefits; whether centralizing the process of setting standards would yield savings in administrative costs; and the objectives and capabilities of different levels of government. For example, federal policymakers might choose standards that gave greater weight to environmental costs than state standards would, because states' objectives include competing with each other for industries and jobs.

Methods of Meeting Those Standards

There is a stronger rationale for a state or local role, rather than a federal one, in deciding which methods may be used to meet environmental standards if the opportunities and costs of available methods vary among areas. For example, the cost of addressing water quality concerns associated with hydraulic fracturing can vary by locality,

depending in part on whether local geology allows producers to dispose of wastewater in underground disposal wells; a federal decision to require that method of disposal might therefore be overly costly in some areas.

Another consideration is whether a particular method of meeting environmental standards would be more cost-effective if it was put to use on a large scale; if so, the argument for federal regulation is stronger. That argument is also stronger when a method of meeting environmental standards would have effects outside the state in which it was used. And constraints on states' willingness and ability to select efficient methods of meeting standards would likewise argue for federal regulation, just as such constraints on local governments would argue for state regulation.

Research

If many states face the same type of environmental problem, a stronger rationale exists for the federal government to determine and fund a research agenda related to that problem. An example is research to determine precisely how much methane is emitted by the development of shale gas, because such research would help inform policies on greenhouse gas emissions in many states and at the federal level. If the endeavor was left to the states, some studies that would be worthwhile to the nation as a whole might not be undertaken, because they would not be justified by the benefits to a single state or even a small group of them. Further, research conducted by one state might be duplicated by another if the states failed to coordinate plans or share findings.

The Basis of CBO's Estimates of Longer-Term Effects on Economic Output

The Congressional Budget Office (CBO) estimates that real (inflation-adjusted) gross domestic product (GDP) will be 0.7 percent higher in 2020 and 0.9 percent higher in 2040 than it would have been without the development of shale resources. The analysis underlying those estimates involved two main steps:

- CBO compared a recent energy market projection by the Energy Information Administration (EIA) in which shale resources were available in the United States to an alternative projection by CBO in which those resources were not available. CBO estimated energy prices and quantities for that alternative projection by extrapolating from EIA's estimates of the effects on energy markets of differences in future amounts of shale energy production.

- Using the two sets of projections, CBO estimated the impact that different quantities and prices in energy markets would have on GDP, focusing on increases in the productivity of existing labor and capital and increases in the amount of labor and capital in use.

Oil and Natural Gas Markets With and Without Shale Resources

CBO analyzed the domestic consumption and net exports of oil products (defined here to include fuels derived from petroleum as well as other liquid fuels, such as ethanol, biodiesel, and natural gas plant liquids) and of natural gas in the projections with and without shale resources, as well as the market prices of oil and natural gas in those two projections. The analysis also took account of the profitability of shale development in the projection that included shale resources. In addition, CBO constructed alternative cases to account for uncertainty about future production levels, energy prices, and profitability of shale gas production.

Consumption and Net Exports of Oil and Natural Gas With and Without Shale Resources

The absence of shale resources would reduce the overall domestic production of oil and natural gas, as well as the domestic use and net exports of natural gas and oil products. However, the magnitudes of those effects differ: CBO estimates that 60 percent of a reduction in the amount of domestic shale gas produced would be reflected in lower domestic gas consumption, that roughly 5 percent would be met by an increase in the production of natural gas not from shale, and that the remaining 35 percent would be reflected in lower exports or higher imports. In contrast, CBO estimates that only 10 percent of a reduction in the amount of tight oil produced would take the form of lower domestic oil consumption, that roughly 20 percent would reflect an increase in the domestic production of crude oil from other sources, and that about 70 percent would be absorbed by greater net imports.[1]

---

1. In this appendix, references to tight oil include not only crude oil that is extracted from shale by means of hydraulic fracturing but also CBO's estimate of the portion of the production of natural gas plant liquids—forms of natural gas that substitute for certain petroleum products—that is produced by hydraulic fracturing. Increased production of shale gas sometimes causes more natural gas plant liquids to be produced, increasing supplies of liquid fuels.

Those values are averages of the values resulting from EIA's estimates of the sensitivities of future consumption levels to the availability of shale energy production.[2] Differences in market size explain the different effects. Because overseas transport to and from North America is more costly for natural gas than for crude oil, U.S. production of shale gas has a comparatively large effect on North American gas prices and thus a comparatively large effect on U.S. gas consumption. In contrast, U.S. production of tight oil has a comparatively small effect on world oil prices, so changes in that production have a relatively small effect on domestic oil consumption and are primarily reflected in changes in net exports.[3]

Thus, given EIA's baseline projection that shale gas production will be about 9.5 trillion cubic feet (Tcf) in 2014, CBO projects that in the absence of that production, total domestic gas production would be about 9.0 Tcf lower (because conventional production would increase by about 0.5 Tcf), domestic consumption would be about 5.5 Tcf lower (roughly 60 percent of 9.5 Tcf), and net exports would be about 3.5 Tcf lower (through lower exports or higher imports). CBO similarly estimates that the domestic production, consumption, and net exports of oil products would all be lower in 2014— by 3.9 million, 0.5 million, and 3.4 million barrels per day, respectively—in the absence of the estimated 4.8 million barrels per day of liquid fuels attributable to shale development.[4] CBO's projections of the production

and consumption of oil and natural gas with and without shale resources are shown in Figure B-1.

Market Prices of Oil and Natural Gas With and Without Shale Resources

Given the estimated differences in the domestic consumption of oil products and natural gas with and without shale resources, the differences in market prices supporting those consumption levels can be calculated by using the elasticity of demand for those fuels. Elasticities measure the percentage change in the production or the consumption of a good for each 1 percent change in the price. Given the estimated reduction in consumption when shale resources are not available (measured relative to the baseline projection, in which they are available), the percentage difference in market prices ($\%\Delta P$) is given by the following equation:

$$\%\Delta P = \frac{\%\Delta D}{\varepsilon_d}$$

In that equation, $\%\Delta D$ refers to the percentage difference in the consumption of oil products or natural gas, and ε_d is the elasticity of demand with respect to differences in the market price of oil or gas.

On the basis of EIA's most recent long-term outlook, CBO estimates the long-term elasticities of demand for oil products and for natural gas to be about -0.5 each, so that a 20 percent increase in the price of oil products or natural gas would reduce the amount of oil and gas consumed by 0.5 times as much, or 10 percent. For instance, domestic gas consumption in 2040 would be about 11.5 Tcf lower in the absence of shale supplies, CBO estimates; that 11.5 Tcf is about 35 percent of 2040 domestic consumption in the baseline projection, implying that gas prices (given the elasticity of demand) would be about 70 percent higher without shale supplies, as Figure B-2 shows. Again, U.S. production of tight oil will have a smaller effect on world prices, which would be about 5 percent higher otherwise, because U.S. tight oil as a share of world liquid fuel supplies is much smaller than U.S. shale gas as a share of North American gas supplies.

---

2. Energy Information Administration, *Annual Energy Outlook 2014 With Projections to 2040*, DOE/EIA-0383(2014) (April 2014), http://go.usa.gov/8KyF (PDF, 12 MB). The estimates are based on changes in the consumption of gas or of total liquid fuels relative to changes in the production of shale gas or tight oil between EIA's "low-resource scenario" and its baseline case. CBO's estimate reflects the five-year average of those ratios from 2036 to 2040 to control for any year-to-year variability and to reflect longer-term conditions stemming from the historical absence of shale resources (rather than the near-term effects that would result from a sudden increase or decrease in the availability of shale resources).

3. Although sensitivities at a moment in time are not directly comparable with changes that occur over time, CBO's estimated effects are qualitatively consistent with the fact that observed consumption levels have not grown as fast as shale energy production, in part because of decreases in conventional production. For instance, from 2001 to 2013, U.S. shale gas production increased by 9 trillion cubic feet (Tcf) per year, conventional gas production fell by 4.5 Tcf, and gas consumption increased by 3.5 Tcf. See Energy Information Administration, *Annual Energy Outlook 2014 With Projections to 2040*, DOE/EIA-0383(2014) (April 2014), http://go.usa.gov/8KyF (PDF, 12 MB).

---

4. The estimate of 4.8 million barrels per day in 2014 consists of EIA's projected tight oil production—about 4.1 million barrels per day—and 0.7 million of the 2.5 million barrels per day that EIA projects for natural gas plant liquids. The remaining 1.8 million barrels per day of natural gas plant liquids correspond to the average production of those liquids from 2006 to 2009, just before the boom in shale gas and tight oil production. See EIA's *Annual Energy Outlook* for 2014 and for 2006 through 2009.

Figure B-1.

Effects of Shale Resources on the Domestic Production and Consumption of Natural Gas and Liquid Fuels

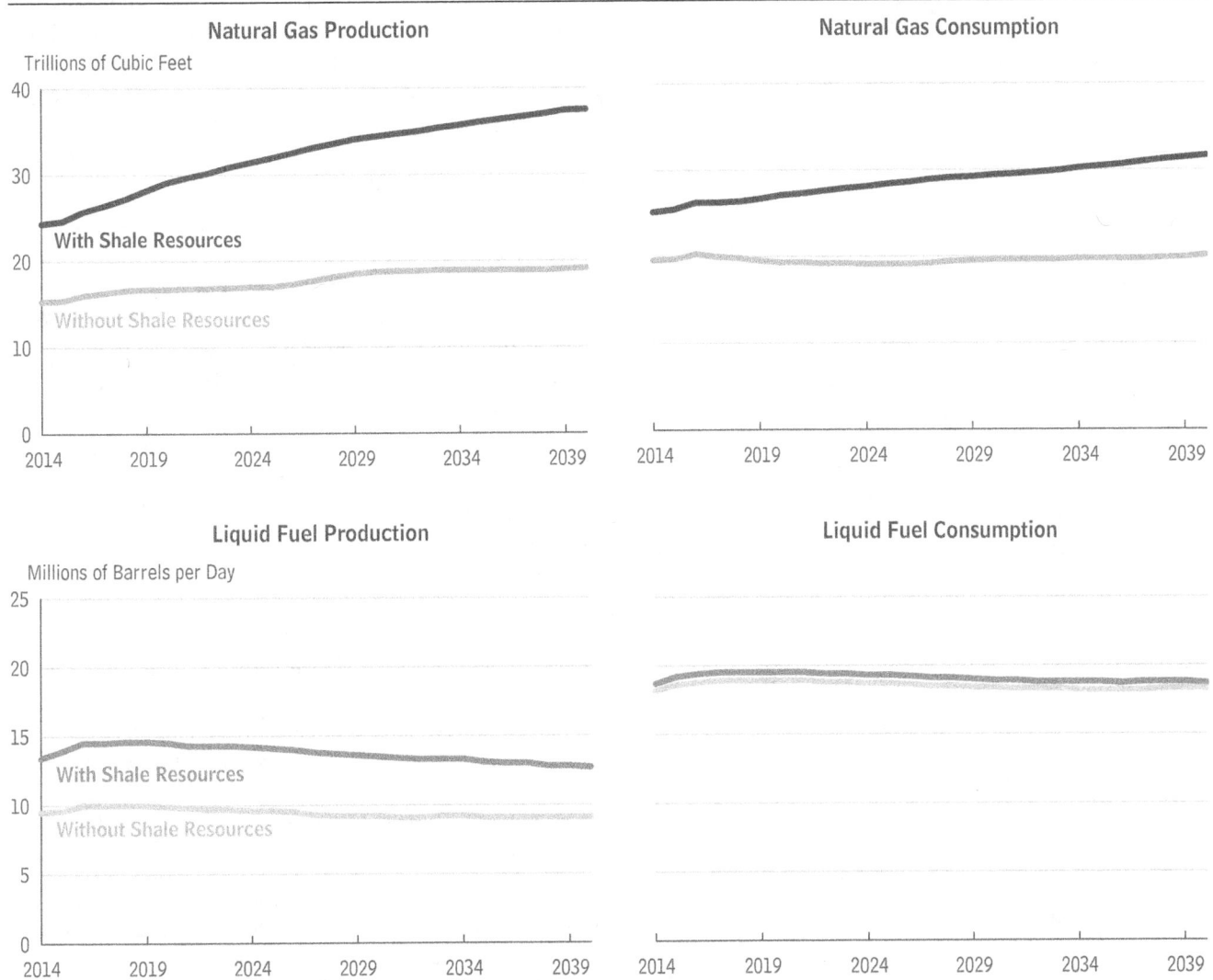

Source: Congressional Budget Office based on Energy Information Administration, *Annual Energy Outlook 2014 With Projections to 2040*, DOE/EIA-0383(2014) (April 2014), http://go.usa.gov/8KyF (PDF, 12 MB).

Notes: Production and consumption amounts for natural gas and liquid fuels when shale resources are present (labeled "With Shale Resources") are the Energy Information Administration's most recent long-term projections. Projections when shale resources are not present (labeled "Without Shale Resources") are CBO's estimates.

The category "Liquid Fuel" includes crude oil, biofuels, natural gas plant liquids, and other liquid fuels.

The projections for all years are based on the assumptions that the economy is producing close to its maximum sustainable level of output and that energy markets are stable. As the text explains, CBO expects that the actual effects would be somewhat different in the short term.

Figure B-2.

Effects of Shale Resources on the Price of Natural Gas and Liquid Fuels

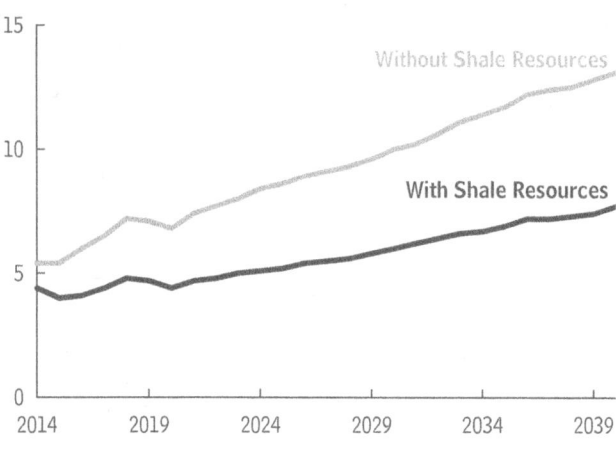

Price of Natural Gas
2012 Dollars per Million British Thermal Units

Without Shale Resources

With Shale Resources

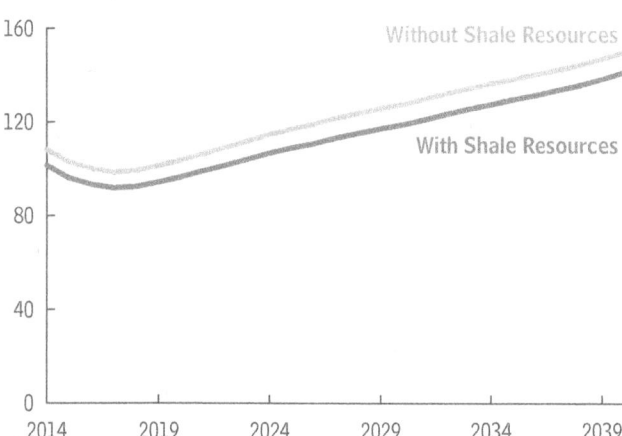

Price of Liquid Fuels
2012 Dollars per Barrel

Without Shale Resources

With Shale Resources

Source: Congressional Budget Office based on Energy Information Administration, *Annual Energy Outlook 2014 With Projections to 2040*, DOE/EIA-0383(2014) (April 2014), http://go.usa.gov/8KyF (PDF, 12 MB).

Notes: Market prices for natural gas and liquid fuels when shale resources are present (labeled "With Shale Resources") are the Energy Information Administration's (EIA's) most recent long-term projections. Projections when shale resources are not present (labeled "Without Shale Resources") are CBO's estimates. CBO reports prices in 2012 dollars because that was the basis that EIA used when modeling its projections in real (inflation-adjusted) terms.

The category "Liquid Fuels" includes crude oil, biofuels, natural gas plant liquids, and other liquid fuels.

The projections for all years are based on the assumptions that the economy is producing close to its maximum sustainable level of output and that energy markets are stable. As the text explains, CBO expects that the actual effects would be somewhat different in the short term.

Combining those estimated price effects with estimates of production volumes, CBO calculates that the value of U.S. oil and gas production in 2020 in the absence of shale development would be about $495 billion (measured in 2012 dollars), as opposed to $645 billion with shale development.[5] In 2040, the value of U.S. oil and gas production would be roughly $760 billion without shale development, as opposed to $950 billion with it.

Profitability of Shale Development

Excess returns from producing shale resources—that is, revenues less production costs—contribute to GDP. They represent the difference between the output of labor and capital when used to produce shale resources and the output of that labor and capital when used elsewhere in the economy.[6] Those excess returns are determined by the volume of tight oil and shale gas expected to be produced in future years and the difference between the market prices of oil and natural gas and the average break-even cost of producing shale resources—that is, the lowest average price necessary for developers of shale resources to cover their costs of labor and capital.

CBO's estimates of the current and future break-even costs of tight oil and shale gas production are based on recent estimates from the International Energy Agency (IEA).[7] IEA estimates that current production costs of tight oil worldwide range from $60 to $100 per barrel

---

5.   In CBO's baseline projection, in which shale resources are assumed to be available, 29.1 Tcf of gas are expected to be produced in the United States during 2020 at a price of $4.40 per million British thermal units (mmBtu). Because there are roughly 1.03 mmBtu in each thousand cubic feet (mcf) of gas and 1 Tcf equals 1 billion mcf, sales of natural gas will total about $130 billion (29.1 multiplied by 1.03 multiplied by $4.40 multiplied by 1 billion). With total liquid fuel production expected to be 14.5 million barrels per day and an oil price of $97 per barrel (assumed to be the same for nonpetroleum fuels), sales of liquid fuels are expected to total about $1.4 billion per day (14.5 million multiplied by $97), or $515 billion per year. In the absence of shale resources, CBO projects, 2020 gas and oil prices would be $6.90 per mmBtu and $103 per barrel; U.S. gas and oil production would be 16.7 Tcf and 9.9 million barrels per day; and total spending on natural gas and liquid fuels would be about $495 billion.

6.   The labor and capital used to produce shale energy include what is used to produce goods and services subsequently employed in shale development—for example, the labor and capital used to produce the concrete that, in turn, provides the casing of a new well.

7.   International Energy Agency, *Resources to Reserves 2013: Oil, Gas and Coal Technologies for the Energy Markets of the Future* (IEA, 2013), www.iea.org/w/bookshop/add.aspx?id=447.

(in 2013 dollars). CBO estimates that the average break-even cost of U.S. tight oil is the midpoint of IEA's range of world costs—that is, $80 per barrel. That figure is consistent with the fact that the production of U.S. tight oil became significant in the last few years, as world oil prices climbed past $100 per barrel. For shale gas, CBO estimates that the current break-even production cost in the United States is $3 per million British thermal units (mmBtu), at the low end of IEA's worldwide range of $3 to $10 per mmBtu (in 2013 dollars). One reason for that estimate is that investment in shale gas in the United States has remained robust even as gas prices have fallen below $4 per mmBtu. Another reason is that world production of shale gas has been concentrated in the United States; domestic production costs are probably lower than in countries where development is proceeding more slowly.

CBO expects that break-even costs will grow in real terms as real prices for oil and gas grow. As market prices rise, companies will develop shale gas and tight oil that are more costly to produce, thereby raising the average cost of production. Specifically, CBO models the average break-even cost for tight oil as growing at the same rate at which real prices for crude oil do, so that the inflation-adjusted break-even cost grows from $80 per barrel in 2014 to about $110 per barrel by 2040. For shale gas, however, CBO models the inflation-adjusted break-even cost as growing at half the rate expected for the real price of natural gas, so that the real break-even cost grows from $3 per mmBtu in 2014 to about $4 per mmBtu by 2040. CBO's different expectations for shale gas and tight oil are broadly consistent with EIA projections that shale gas production will grow as a share of total U.S. gas production in coming decades because it will become relatively cheaper, while tight oil's share of total U.S. production of liquid fuels will not change significantly.

CBO estimates that inflation-adjusted excess returns in 2020 will total roughly $20 billion for shale gas, an estimate based on about 13 Tcf of production, a price of $4.40 per mmBtu, and a break-even cost of $2.90 per mmBtu. CBO also estimates—on the basis of about 5.6 million barrels per day of expected production, a price of $97 per barrel, and a break-even cost of $75 per barrel—that inflation-adjusted excess returns in 2020 will total $45 billion for tight oil. In 2040, CBO expects inflation-adjusted excess returns to total about $75 billion for shale gas and $50 billion for tight oil.

Uncertainty About Projections

Shale energy production, market prices of gas and oil, and the profitability of shale gas production may be significantly higher or lower than CBO projects in its baseline. All things being equal, higher production, market prices, and profitability would mean larger effects on GDP. To illustrate the uncertainty accompanying its baseline estimates, CBO generated alternative projections of those three factors.

CBO constructed a range of shale production quantities on the basis of a recent EIA "low-resource" projection in which the total amount of gas and oil recoverable from each shale gas and tight oil well was 50 percent lower than in EIA's baseline projection.[8] Comparing the two projections, CBO calculated the percentage difference in the number of Btus of shale gas and tight oil produced each year. CBO then obtained its range of shale production quantities by increasing or decreasing its baseline projections for shale gas and tight oil production by those year-by-year percentages.[9] The resulting percentage deviations from baseline production levels are shown in Figure B-3.

To generate alternative projections of market prices, CBO relied on EIA's most recent long-term outlook, which includes projections for higher and lower oil prices. (CBO used the market price of crude oil to approximate the price of liquid fuels, which include crude oil, the petroleum products produced from it, and other liquids, such as biofuels and natural gas plant liquids.) In the absence of analogous EIA projections for natural gas prices, CBO used the same percentage increase and decrease (relative to the baseline projections) that it did for the price of oil. The high and low prices that CBO obtained for natural gas and oil are shown in Figure B-4.

---

8. See the low-resource scenario in Energy Information Administration, *Annual Energy Outlook 2014 With Projections to 2040*, DOE/EIA-0383(2014) (April 2014), http://go.usa.gov/8KyF (PDF, 12 MB). The actual production of shale gas and tight oil in that scenario falls by less than 50 percent because the effects of the decline take some time to materialize and because higher market prices promote the development of additional wells.

9. EIA also analyzed a high-resource scenario in which shale gas and tight oil wells were more productive than they were in the agency's baseline projection. CBO did not use that scenario to calculate any of its range of shale production quantities because the scenario included changes to *conventional* oil and gas supplies that were not included in EIA's low-resource scenario.

Figure B-3.

Projected High and Low Production of Shale Gas and Tight Oil

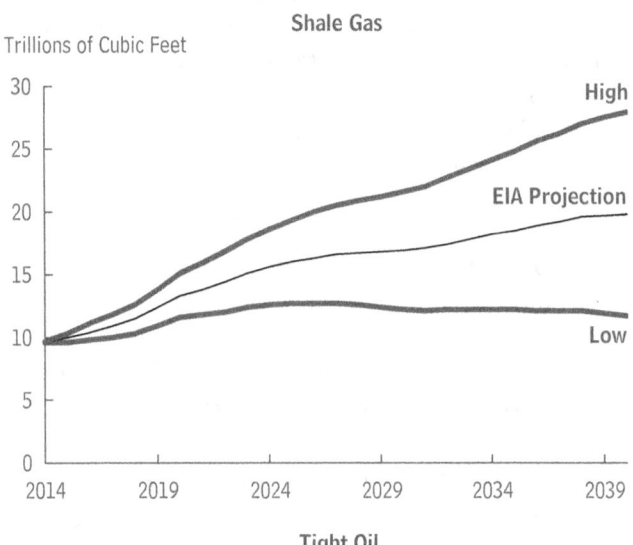

Shale Gas

Trillions of Cubic Feet

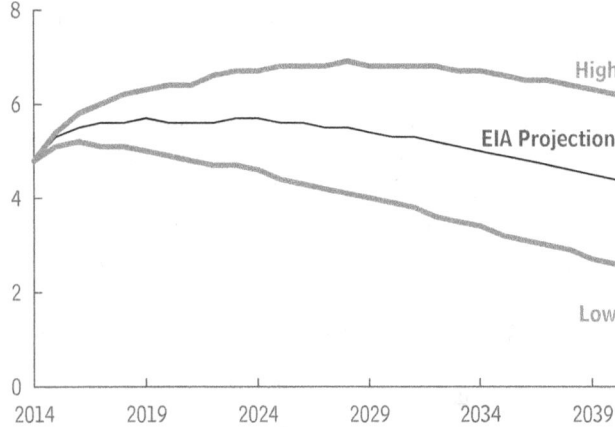

Tight Oil

Millions of Barrels per Day

Source: Congressional Budget Office based on Energy Information Administration, *Annual Energy Outlook 2014 With Projections to 2040*, DOE/EIA-0383(2014) (April 2014), http://go.usa.gov/8KyF (PDF, 12 MB).

Notes: Here, the production of tight oil includes not only crude oil that is extracted from shale by means of hydraulic fracturing but also CBO's estimate of the portion of the production of natural gas plant liquids—forms of natural gas that substitute for certain petroleum products—that is produced by hydraulic fracturing.

EIA = Energy Information Administration.

To measure the sensitivity of CBO's findings to the profitability of producing shale gas, CBO considered cases in which break-even costs for shale gas grew at 25 percent and 75 percent of the yearly change in gas prices, rather than the 50 percent assumed in the baseline projection.

In dollar terms, excess returns from shale gas production are greatest if the market price of gas is high and the break-even cost of production is low; conversely, excess returns are smallest if the market price of gas is low and the break-even cost is high.

When evaluating the effects of greater or lesser availability of shale energy supplies, CBO included price effects resulting from those differences in supplies. For any given assumption about other factors affecting prices—whether those factors lead to high prices, baseline prices, or low prices—more abundant shale energy supplies will, all else being equal, reduce those prices. Similarly, those prices will be higher if supplies are less abundant. CBO used the same approach that was outlined above to calculate the effect of more or less shale production on those price scenarios: More (or less) abundant shale gas or tight oil boosts (or lowers) consumption levels, leading to a percentage change in market prices that is calculated by means of the elasticity of demand.

Effects of Shale Development on Economic Output in the Longer Term

Real GDP will be higher in the longer term than it would have been without the development of shale resources. CBO estimates that, by increasing the productivity of labor and capital, the production and use of shale gas will make GDP about 0.2 percent higher in 2020 and about 0.4 percent higher in 2040 than it would have been otherwise, and the production and use of tight oil will make GDP about 0.2 percent higher in both of those years (see Table B-1). Moreover, because that higher productivity of labor and capital will induce a greater supply of labor and capital in the economy, shale development will further increase GDP by roughly 0.3 percent and 0.4 percent in 2020 and 2040, respectively. All told, CBO's baseline long-term projection for real GDP is 0.7 percent higher in 2020 and 0.9 percent higher in 2040 than it would have been without the development of shale resources.[10]

CBO's analysis focused on the effects on GDP in the longer term—that is, after the economy moves back toward producing its maximum sustainable level of output. In the near term, the increase in GDP associated with

10. Because of rounding, the total change in real GDP is slightly less than the sum of the component changes.

Figure B-4.

Projected High and Low Market Prices of Natural Gas and Oil

Natural Gas

2012 Dollars per Million British Thermal Units

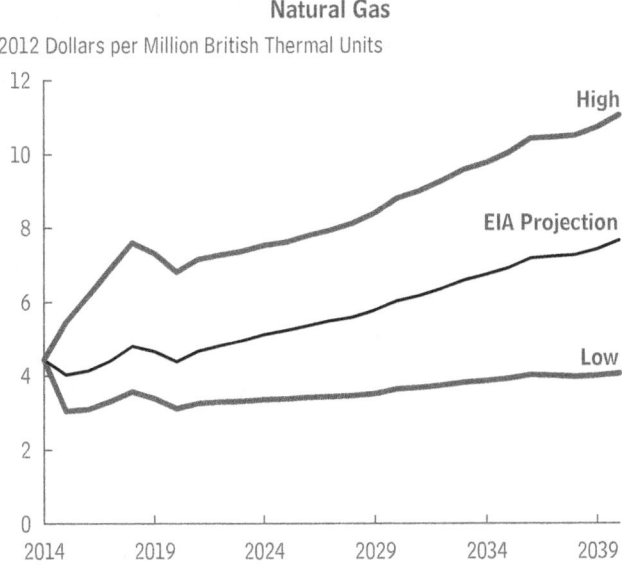

Oil

2012 Dollars per Barrel

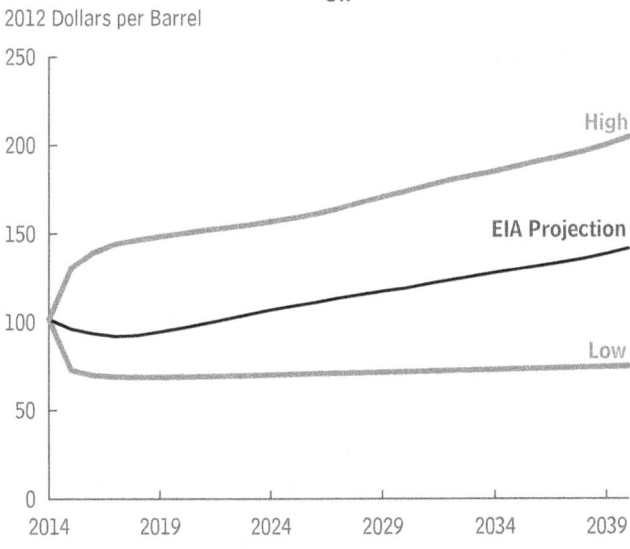

Source: Congressional Budget Office based on Energy Information Administration, *Annual Energy Outlook 2014 With Projections to 2040*, DOE/EIA-0383(2014) (April 2014), http://go.usa.gov/8KyF (PDF, 12 MB).

Notes: CBO reports prices in 2012 dollars because that was the basis that EIA used when modeling its projections in real (inflation-adjusted) terms.

EIA = Energy Information Administration.

increased production and use of shale resources is greater because the firms producing and using more shale resources use some labor and capital that would otherwise have been underused. For example, in the current economic environment, some of the workers employed by businesses engaged in hydraulic fracturing would otherwise have been unemployed. In the economic environment that CBO expects in the long run, however, such workers would otherwise have been employed in other jobs.

Effects of Shale Gas on the Productivity of Labor and Capital

To think about the long-term effects of shale gas on productivity and hence on GDP, consider Figure B-5 on page 39, which shows two hypothetical supply curves for natural gas: one that does not include shale gas and one that does. The supply curve without shale gas is line S1, and it intersects the demand curve for natural gas—line D—at point A, showing that without shale gas, the market for natural gas would clear (that is, demand would equal supply) at a price of $4 per thousand cubic feet (mcf).[11] Once shale gas becomes available, the total supply of natural gas shifts to S2, meaning that more gas is available at a lower price. The horizontal difference between S1 and S2 is the amount of shale gas supplied at a given price. For example, at a price of $3 per mcf, the supply of shale gas is the horizontal difference between the quantities represented by points E and B. The market now clears at point B, at a price of $3.

The gain in GDP in the long run from that outward shift of the supply curve closely corresponds to the area enclosed by points A, B, and C. The gain is composed of three parts:

■ The gain from the increased productivity of labor and capital used to produce shale gas, which corresponds to the area enclosed by points B, C, and E;

---

11. The market that determines the domestic price of natural gas includes supply and demand in Canada and Mexico. To focus on the effects on GDP in the United States, the reader should interpret the supply curves, S1 and S2, as representing domestic supply, and the demand curve, D, as representing demand net of supplies from Canada and Mexico.

Table B-1.

Effects of U.S. Shale Development on GDP

Percent

	Effect on GDP	
	2020	2040
Increased Productivity of Labor and Capital		
Shale gas		
Gain in productivity of labor and capital producing shale gas	0.1	0.3
Gain in productivity from producing shale gas instead of conventional gas	*	*
Gain in productivity from increased consumption of gas	0.1	0.1
Subtotal	0.2	0.4
Tight oil		
Gain in productivity of labor and capital producing tight oil	0.2	0.2
Gain in productivity from producing tight oil instead of conventional oil	*	*
Gain in productivity from increased consumption of oil	*	*
Subtotal	0.2	0.2
Total	0.4	0.5
Additional Supply of Labor and Capital	0.3	0.4
Total Effect of U.S. Shale Development on GDP	**0.7**	**0.9**
Memorandum:[a]		
Gains in Productivity of Labor and Capital Producing Shale Resources	0.3	0.4
Gains in Productivity From Producing Shale Resources Instead of Conventional Resources	*	*
Gains in Productivity From Increased Consumption of Gas and Oil	0.1	0.1

Source: Congressional Budget Office.

Notes: Totals may not match because of rounding.

Tight oil is crude oil extracted from shale and certain other dense rock formations by means of hydraulic fracturing.

GDP = gross domestic product; * = between zero and 0.05 percent.

a. These lines add shale gas's effects on GDP (shown above in the table) to tight oil's effects on GDP (also shown above in the table).

■ The gain in productivity from producing shale gas instead of more expensive conventional gas, which corresponds to the triangle with corners at points A, E, and F; and

■ The gain in productivity from the increased consumption of gas by domestic businesses and households, which is included in the area enclosed by points A, B, and F.[12]

---

12. The area enclosed by points A, B, and F also includes the gain to foreign users that are able to consume more natural gas. In calculating the gains to U.S. GDP, CBO considered only the changes in domestic consumption.

Gains From the Increased Productivity of Labor and Capital Producing Shale Gas. In the longer run, the development of shale gas leads to higher GDP in part because labor and capital can be used more productively to produce shale gas than to produce other output. In Figure B-5, that gain is shown by the area between the two supply curves and below $3 per mcf—the triangle bounded by points B, C, and E. In Figure B-6, the same gain is shown by the area above the supply curve S3—which is a supply curve for shale gas alone—and below $3; it is also a triangle bounded by points B, C, and E. (The distance from B to E in Figure B-5 represents the quantity of shale gas produced at the new equilibrium price—the same quantity represented by the distance from B to E in Figure B-6. The areas of the two triangles bounded by points B, C, and E in the two figures are the same because their bases and heights are the same.)

Figure B-5.

Hypothetical Long-Run Market for Natural Gas

Price (Dollars per thousand cubic feet)

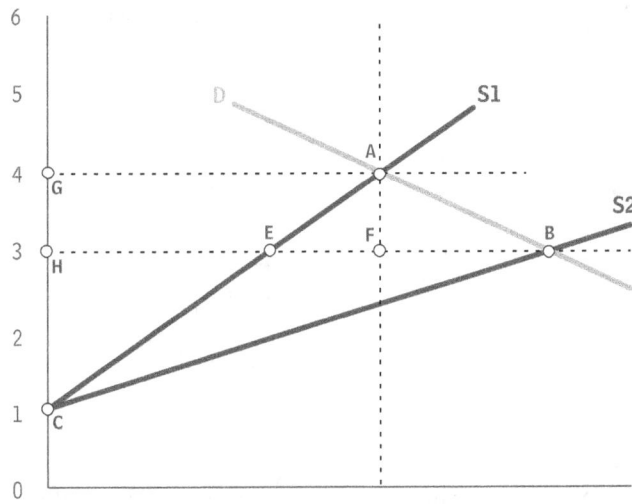

Production and Consumption

Source: Congressional Budget Office.

Note: Line D is the hypothetical demand curve for natural gas produced in the United States. Lines S1 and S2 are the supply curves for natural gas without and with shale resources. Points A and B denote the price and quantity of natural gas produced in the United States in those two cases.

At any point along S3 in Figure B-6, the addition to GDP from the production of shale gas is the vertical distance between the supply curve and the price of gas. For example, at point C, a firm is willing to supply shale gas at a long-run price of $1 per mcf or more because the cost of labor and capital used by that firm to produce 1 mcf of gas is $1. That $1 of labor and capital would be producing $1 of GDP if employed in other industries. At a price of $3, the shift of labor and capital from other industries generates an extra $2 of GDP, the vertical difference between points C and E. To take another example: At point B of Figure B-6, the production of an additional 1 mcf of shale gas is profitable only if the long-run price is $3 or more. Because the labor and capital used to produce that gas could produce $3 of GDP elsewhere, there is no net gain in GDP from the production of shale gas that is also valued at $3.

Another way to think about the gain in GDP from the production of shale gas is to subtract the total cost of producing shale gas from the total value of that gas. The cost is the quantity of gas produced multiplied by the

break-even cost, and it is shown by the area enclosed by points B, C, J, and K in Figure B-6. The value of the gas produced is its price multiplied by the quantity produced, which is shown by the rectangle whose corners are points B, E, J, and K. The difference is represented by the triangle enclosed by points B, C, and E.

CBO estimated the long-term gain in GDP from the production of shale gas by multiplying its estimate of the amount of shale gas produced (which would correspond to the distance between points B and E in Figure B-6, though that figure, again, is hypothetical) by the difference between the price of that gas and CBO's estimate of the average break-even cost of that production (which would be equivalent to the vertical midpoint of the supply curve between points B and C). CBO estimates the GDP gain from the production of shale gas to be 0.1 percent of GDP in 2020 and 0.3 percent in 2040. In 2012 dollars, the 2040 estimate is about $75 billion, which is based on projections that shale gas production in 2040 will total about 20 billion mcf; that the market price of gas will be about $8 per mcf; and that the average break-even cost of shale gas will be about $4 per mcf.

Figure B-6.

Hypothetical Long-Run Supply Curve for Shale Gas

Price (Dollars per thousand cubic feet)

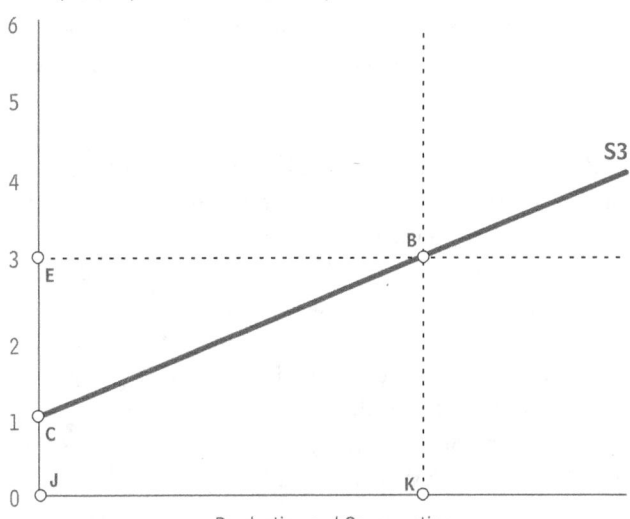

Production and Consumption

Source: Congressional Budget Office.

Note: Line S3 is the supply curve for shale gas. Point B denotes the quantity of shale gas produced in the United States at a price of $3 per thousand cubic feet.

The gains in GDP from producing shale gas are greater in the near term than in the long term. When labor and capital are underused, some of the resources used to produce shale gas would not otherwise be producing GDP. In that case, the gain to GDP from producing shale gas is represented not only by the triangle enclosed by points B, C, and E in Figure B-6 but also by part of the area enclosed by points B, C, J, and K.

Gains in Productivity From Producing Shale Gas Instead of Conventional Gas. The gain in GDP from substituting shale gas for conventional gas that is no longer economical to produce because of the lower price of gas corresponds to the triangle enclosed by points A, E, and F in Figure B-5. A firm willing to supply additional conventional gas at point A requires a price of $4 per mcf because it uses $4 of labor and capital. Displacing that conventional gas with shale gas produced at a cost of $3 thus frees up $1 of labor and capital for other uses, increasing GDP by $1. A firm willing to supply additional conventional gas at point E uses $3 of labor and capital to produce that gas, so replacing it with shale gas at $3 per mcf does not add to GDP.

The savings that consumers of natural gas realize because of the fall in price from $4 to $3 is represented by the rectangle enclosed by points A, F, H, and G in Figure B-5. Most of those savings do not add to GDP but instead represent a transfer from producers to consumers of natural gas. Within that rectangle, only the savings in production costs, which are represented by the triangle outlined by points A, E, and F, add to GDP.

CBO estimated the gain in GDP from substituting shale gas for conventional gas by multiplying the estimated difference in U.S. production of conventional gas by one-half the difference between the projected price of gas and the estimated price that would prevail in the absence of shale resources. The gain in GDP is projected to be very small in both 2020 and 2040—less than 0.05 percent of GDP—because the production of conventional gas is expected to be only about 5 percent lower than it would have been without shale resources.

Gains in Productivity From Increased Consumption of Gas. The development of shale resources also raises GDP as consumption of cheaper gas frees up labor and capital for other uses, allowing the economy to produce a greater value of goods and services with the same total amount of labor and capital. In Figure B-5, those gains are included

in the triangle enclosed by points A, B, and F. (That triangle also includes gains to foreign firms that use more natural gas. Those gains do not contribute to U.S. GDP, and CBO excluded them from its calculations.)

As the price of natural gas falls, productivity increases for two reasons. First, some firms are able to reduce their cost of producing goods and services by substituting cheaper gas for labor, capital, or other inputs. For example, an electric utility might generate more electricity from gas and less from coal. Second, the composition of output produced in the economy changes as households and firms shift toward goods and services that are gas-intensive and thus become relatively less costly to produce. For example, households might buy more tires, fertilizer, and plastic containers, and spend less on clothes.

In both cases, the benefit to the economy of each additional thousand cubic feet of natural gas used is the difference between the highest price at which that gas would be purchased, represented by the heights of the points along demand curve D in Figure B-5, and its actual selling price. Consider, for example, an electric utility willing to buy an additional 1 mcf of natural gas at a price up to $4—the level of demand represented by point A in the figure. That willingness to spend up to $4 reflects the utility's ability to substitute the gas—as well as the costs of using it—for other resources that together cost the same amount. For instance, the utility might buy 1 mcf of gas costing $4, plus $5 of other necessary goods and services, to generate electricity that was previously generated from coal at the same total cost of $9. If, instead, the gas costs $3, producing electricity with gas instead of coal reduces the utility's costs by $1 (the distance between points A and F), and the $1 of labor and capital that is no longer needed to generate electricity can produce an additional $1 of output elsewhere in the economy.[13] Additional consumption of natural gas by firms whose demand is represented by points between A and B on the demand curve would free up smaller amounts of labor and capital, and GDP would increase by amounts

---

13. The utility itself might not reduce its use of labor and capital, but those resources would be freed up elsewhere in the economy—particularly in coal production and related activities. Note that the effect on the *composition* of GDP exceeds the effect on its size: In this hypothetical situation, the output of the natural gas industry increases by $3 and GDP increases by $1.

Figure B-7.

Hypothetical Long-Run Market for Crude Oil in the United States

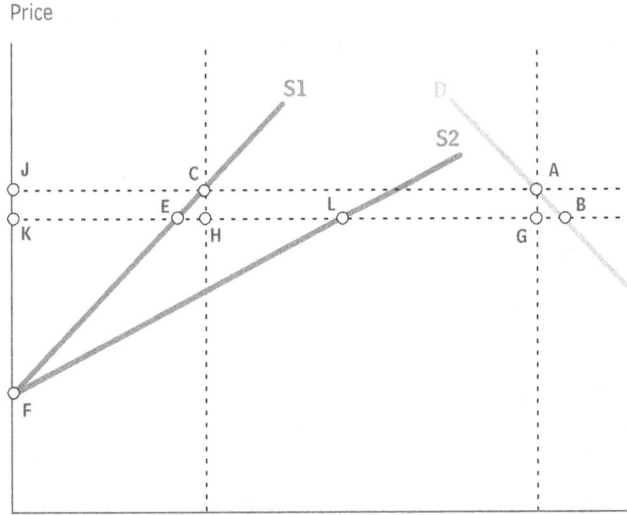

Source: Congressional Budget Office.

Note: Line D is the hypothetical demand curve for crude oil consumed in the United States. Lines S1 and S2 are the domestic supply curves for crude oil without and with shale resources. Points A and B denote the price and quantity of crude oil consumed in the United States in those two cases. Points C and L denote the price and quantity of crude oil supplied by U.S. producers in those two cases.

between $1 and zero for each additional 1 mcf of gas used.

Similar logic applies in the case of shifts in demand toward goods and services that are more gas-intensive. For an additional unit of a gas-intensive product, a household or firm at point A is willing to pay $4 per mcf for the natural gas that went into making the product, plus the other costs of the product, instead of spending the same total amount on other goods or services. If natural gas costs $4 per mcf, then such a shift does not increase GDP, though it does change GDP's composition: The same total quantity of resources not used to produce the goods or services forgone is used to produce the additional unit of the gas-intensive product. If natural gas instead costs $3 per mcf to produce, the buyer's shift to the gas-intensive product reduces the total production costs of the goods purchased, and each additional 1 mcf used frees up $1 of resources that can produce additional GDP.

CBO estimated the gain in GDP by multiplying the estimated change in U.S. consumption of gas by one-half the difference between the projected price of gas and the estimated price that would prevail in the absence of shale resources. The gain in GDP is projected to be 0.1 percent in 2020 and also in 2040.

Effects of Tight Oil on the Productivity of Labor and Capital

The effects on GDP of the domestic production of tight oil differ from those of the domestic production of shale gas because oil is traded in a global market. Thus, most of the gains from greater consumption of tight oil will occur outside the United States. However, all of the gains from using labor and capital more productively to produce tight oil than they could be used for other purposes will add to U.S. GDP—by 0.2 percent of GDP in 2020 and 2040, CBO estimates.

Gains From the Increased Productivity of Labor and Capital Producing Tight Oil. The gains in GDP associated with using labor and capital to produce tight oil instead of other goods and services are illustrated in Figure B-7. The availability of tight oil shifts the supply curve of all U.S. crude oil from S1 to S2. The price of oil, established in the world oil market (which is not shown), falls from point J to point K. As a result, U.S. consumption of crude oil increases along the demand curve from A to B. The supply of conventional crude oil produced domestically falls from H to E, but the total domestic production of crude oil increases from H to L. Imports of crude oil fall, as the difference between the domestic demand for crude oil and the domestic supply narrows from the distance between A and C to the distance between B and L.

Most of the increase in GDP comes from the fact that labor and capital can be used more productively to produce tight oil than to produce other output. Using the same approach that it used when analyzing shale gas production, CBO estimated the long-term gains in GDP from the production of tight oil by multiplying its estimate of the amount of tight oil produced (which would correspond to the distance between points L and E in Figure B-7) by the difference between the price of that oil (point K) and CBO's estimate of the average break-even cost of that production (which would be equivalent to the midpoint of the supply curve between points F and L). CBO estimates that the production of tight oil will increase GDP by 0.2 percent in 2020 and 2040. In 2012 dollars, the 2040 figure is about $50 billion, which is based on projections of 4.4 million barrels per day (or about 1.6 billion barrels per year) of tight oil production in 2040; a price of roughly $140 per barrel; and an average break-even cost of about $110.

Gains in Productivity From Producing Tight Oil Instead of Conventional Oil. The gain in GDP from substituting tight oil for conventional oil that is no longer economical to produce because of the lower price of oil corresponds to the triangle bounded by points C, E, and H in Figure B-7. CBO estimated that gain in GDP by multiplying its estimate of the change in U.S. production of conventional oil by one-half the difference between the projected price of oil and the hypothetical price in the absence of shale resources. The gain is proportionally much smaller than the analogous gain for shale gas because oil is traded in a global market, which implies that the percentage impact of shale development on world oil prices is much smaller than the percentage impact on U.S. gas prices and thus that the effect on U.S. production of conventional oil is also much smaller. As a result, the effect on GDP will be very small in both 2020 and 2040, CBO projects.

Gains in Productivity From Increased Consumption of Oil. To a small degree, GDP rises as firms substitute cheaper oil for labor and capital and as goods and services produced using oil become cheaper to produce than other goods and services. The gain to GDP is reflected in the triangle bounded by points A, B, and G. Because the production of tight oil will have relatively little impact on the price of crude oil, CBO estimates that U.S. consumption of crude oil will be essentially unchanged and that the effect on GDP will be very small in both 2020 and 2040. (The majority of the gains from using more crude oil will accrue outside the United States.)

Effects of Shale Gas and Tight Oil on the Supplies of Labor and Capital

The increases in GDP associated with increased productivity would spur further increases in GDP by increasing the supplies of labor and capital. As GDP rises, households have more income to save and invest; most of the additional savings are invested domestically. That investment increases the capital stock, thus increasing the economy's productive capacity and raising GDP. In addition, higher labor productivity is reflected in higher wages, which encourage people to work and lead to an increase in the number of hours worked, likewise raising GDP. The two effects reinforce each other: A larger capital stock boosts labor productivity and wages, and an increase in the number of hours worked increases saving and investment.

CBO estimates that those indirect effects of shale development will raise GDP by 0.3 percent in 2020 and by 0.4 percent in 2040. Those estimates are based on projections of an increase of 0.1 percent in the number of hours worked in both years and of increases in the capital stock of 0.7 percent in 2020 and 0.9 percent in 2040. The projected changes in hours worked are derived from CBO's estimate that the elasticity of labor supply is 0.19 (so that a 1 percent increase in GDP per hour worked boosts the labor supply by 0.19 percent).[14] The changes in the capital stock are based on the expectation that saving and investment rise proportionally with output, so that in the long run, the percentage increase in the capital stock is equal to the percentage increase in output. CBO converted the changes in hours worked and capital stock into a change in GDP on the basis of a coefficient for labor in the production function of 0.7 and a coefficient for capital of 0.3.

---

14. Congressional Budget Office, *How the Supply of Labor Responds to Changes in Fiscal Policy* (October 2012), www.cbo.gov/publication/43674. CBO's labor supply elasticity is the sum of its estimates of the substitution elasticity (how much an increase in wages increases the amount of labor supplied because working becomes more valuable relative to other uses of people's time) and of the income elasticity (how much an increase in wages allows people to work fewer hours while maintaining their standard of living).

List of Tables and Figures

Tables

Figures

About This Document

This Congressional Budget Office (CBO) report reflects research undertaken in support of the agency's baseline economic projections, which serve as the basis for its budget projections. In keeping with CBO's mandate to provide objective, impartial analysis, the report makes no recommendations.

Ron Gecan and Natalie Tawil of CBO's Microeconomic Studies Division and Mark Lasky of the Macroeconomic Analysis Division wrote the report, with contributions from Mark Booth of the Tax Analysis Division, Kathleen Gramp and Jeff LaFave of the Budget Analysis Division, and Charles Pineles-Mark of the Health, Retirement, and Long-Term Analysis Division, and with guidance from Perry Beider, Wendy Edelberg, and Joseph Kile. Terry Dinan, Peter Fontaine, Pamela Greene, Teresa Gullo, and Andrew Stocking provided comments.

Philip Budzik of the Energy Information Administration, Ian Duncan of the University of Texas, Jan Hatzius of Goldman Sachs, Robert Howarth of Cornell University, Robert Jackson of Stanford University, Shashank Mohan of Rhodium Group, W. David Montgomery of NERA Economic Consulting, Sreenivas Ramaswamy of McKinsey & Company, and Duane Zavadil of Bill Barrett Corporation also commented. The assistance of external reviewers implies no responsibility for the final product, which rests solely with CBO.

Jeffrey Kling reviewed the report, Benjamin Plotinsky edited it, and Maureen Costantino prepared it for publication. An electronic version is available on CBO's website (www.cbo.gov/publication/49815).

Douglas W. Elmendorf
Director

December 2014

www.ingramcontent.com/pod-product-compliance
Lightning Source LLC
Chambersburg PA
CBHW080623290526
45790CB00007B/2907